Actes du XIVème Congrès UISPP, Université de Liège, Belgique, 2-8 septembre 2001

Acts of the XIVth UISPP Congress, University of Liège, Belgium, 2-8 September 2001

Colloque / Symposium 1.4

L'outillage lithique en contextes ethnoarchéologiques

Lithic Toolkits in Ethnoarchaeological Contexts

Édité par / Edited by

Xavier Terradas

BAR International Series 1370

2005

Published in 2016 by
BAR Publishing, Oxford

BAR International Series 1370

Acts of the XIVth UISPP Congress, University of Liège, Belgium, 2-8 September 2001
Colloque / Symposium 1.4

L'outillage lithique en contextes ethnoarchéologiques / Lithic Toolkits in Ethnoarchaeological Contexts

ISBN 978 1 84171 812 5

© The editors and contributors severally and the Publisher 2005

Avec la collaboration du Ministère de la Région Wallonne.
Direction générale de l'Aménagement du territoire, du Logement et du Patrimoine.
Subvention n°03/15718
Mise en page / Editing : Rebecca MILLER

Marcel OTTE, Secrétaire général du XIVème Congrès de l'U.I.S.P.P.
Université de Liège, Service de Préhistoire
7, place du XX août, bât. A1
4000 Liège Belgique
Tél. 0032/4/366.53.41   Fax 0032/4/366.55.51
Email : prehist@ulg.ac.be Web : http://www.ulg.ac.be/prehist

Typesetting and layout: Darko Jerko

The authors' moral rights under the 1988 UK Copyright,
Designs and Patents Act are hereby expressly asserted.
All rights reserved. No part of this work may be copied, reproduced, stored,
sold, distributed, scanned, saved in any form of digital format or transmitted
in any form digitally, without the written permission of the Publisher.

BAR Publishing is the trading name of British Archaeological Reports (Oxford) Ltd.
British Archaeological Reports was first incorporated in 1974 to publish the BAR
Series, International and British. In 1992 Hadrian Books Ltd became part of the BAR
group. This volume was originally published by Archaeopress in conjunction with
British Archaeological Reports (Oxford) Ltd / Hadrian Books Ltd, the Series principal
publisher, in 2005. This present volume is published by BAR Publishing, 2016.

Printed in England

BAR titles are available from:

        BAR Publishing
        122 Banbury Rd, Oxford, OX2 7BP, UK
EMAIL   info@barpublishing.com
PHONE +44 (0)1865 310431
  FAX   +44 (0)1865 316916
        www.barpublishing.com

TABLE OF CONTENTS / TABLE DES MATIÈRES

COLLOQUE / SYMPOSIUM 1.4
L'outillage lithique en contextes ethnoarchéologiques
Coordinateur / Coordinator: **Xavier Terradas**

Stone Tools In Ethnoarchaeological Contexts:
   Theoretical-Methodological Inferences 1
I. Briz, I. Clemente Conte, J. Pijoan, X. Terradas, A. Vila

Deep Impact: Stones in Bones. Some Thoughts about the
   Ethnoarchaeology Contrast. A View from Tierra Del Fuego
   (Extreme South America) 9
L. Mameli, J. Estévez, E.L. Piana

Obsidienne verte de Feu-Patagonie, ¿son utilisation constante
   pendant 6000 ans? 19
A. Prieto, M. San Roman, F. Morello & C. Stern

Utilisation opportuniste d'outils en pierre chez les Turkana
   (Nord Kenya) 25
J.-P. Brugal, V. Mourre

Reverse Knapping in the Antipodes: The Spatial Implications
   of Alternate Approaches to Knapping 35
P. Hiscock

The Manufacture and Use of Leather Consumption Goods by the
   Yamana of Tunel VII, Northern Coast of Beagle Channel (Argentina):
   An Ethnographic Evaluation and Its Archaeological Comparision 41
I. Clemente Conte

Inferences and Limitations in Chipped-Stone Modeling: Learning from an
   Ethnoarchaeological Case (Threshing-Sledge Production
   in Thessaly, Greece) 47
L. Karimali

Analysis of an Archaeological Grinding Tool: What to Do
   with Archaeological Artefacts 57
D. Zurro, R. Risch, I. Clemente Conte

STONE TOOLS IN ETHNOARCHAEOLOGICAL CONTEXTS: THEORETICAL-METHODOLOGICAL INFERENCES[1]

Ivan BRIZ, Ignacio CLEMENTE, Jordi PIJOAN,
Xavier TERRADAS & Assumpció VILA

Résumé : Avec ce travail nous faisons une révision critique de l'utilisation qu'on a fait des données ethnologiques en la recherche des sociétés préhistoriques et l'étude de son outillage lithique. A partir de cette révision, nous remarquons l'inutilité des analogies ethnographiques formelles, étant donnée son incapacité de générer des explications sur la causalité des ensembles de restes lithiques. De cette façon, nous faisons une contre formulation de la recherche ethnoarchéologique dirigée à l'obtention d'une méthodologie archéologique, ajustée à l'étude de la dynamique socioéconomique des sociétés préhistoriques. Dans ce sens, la recherche ethnoarchéologique que nous venons développé sur des sociétés de chasseurs-cueilleurs de la Terre du Feu en Argentine nous a permis de constater la manque de signification sociale des catégories morphologiques et technologiques habituellement utilisées dans les analyses archéologiques des ensembles lithiques. Finalement, nous proposons des différentes catégories d'analyse afin de pouvoir déterminer les objectives de la production, en reconstruisant et caractérisant les stratégies développées en la gestion des ressources minérales en vue de la manufacture de l'outillage lithique et des autres biens de consommation. L'interaction des différents éléments de la production nous donne la possibilité d'accès à une dimension dynamique et économique du développement de ces stratégies et de leurs résultats matériels.

Abstract: We present a critical review of the use which ethnological data has been used for the study of prehistoric societies and stone tools. In this sense, we note the uselessness of formal ethnographic analogies, in view of their incapacity to generate explanations for the causality of lithic assemblages. In this way, we claim a new formulation of ethnoarchaeological research, focused on developing an archaeological methodology conforming to the study of the socio-economic dynamics of prehistoric societies. Thus, the ethnoarchaeological research we are developing with hunter-gatherers societies from the Tierra del Fuego archipelago (Argentina) permit us to corroborate the lack of social significance of the morphological and technological categories that have been typically used in lithic analyses. It is for this reason that we propose different analytic categories which allow us to determinate the goals of lithic production and, at the same time, to reconstruct and characterize developed strategies in mineral resource management for the production of stone tools and other consumer goods. The interaction between different elements of production makes possible an economic and dynamic approach to the development of these strategies and their material effects.

INTRODUCTION

Traditionally, prehistoric archaeology has concentrated most of its attention, and consequently most of its studies, on assemblages of lithic remains, considering them to be a key element to improve our knowledge of the oldest phases of prehistory. The study of these remains has been given so much importance for two reasons: firstly, because of their constant and abundant presence in the archaeological record, due to their mineral nature, which is more resistant to the processes of post-depositional destruction and alteration and secondly, because of the markedly positivist scientific spirit of the early 20th century, which reduced archaeological studies to the so-called material culture. This reduction of the object of archaeological study meant that attention was even more centred on lithic remains, which was identified as a defining element of prehistoric cultures.

This exaggeration of the importance of lithic remains did not favour the development of suitable methodologies for their study and interpretation. Interest was centred on the description and search for formal similarities and differences among the different elements that made up lithic assemblages in order to create subgroups which could be related to social, chronological and ethnic entities. The parameters that determined formal recurrences were exclusively based on those pieces that had undergone a modification of their original morphology through retouch. These retouched remains were awarded the category of tool, based on the supposition that greater formal complexity implied greater technological complexity. As a result, a series of periodisations were established founded on a variety of typologies of the supposed tools and groups of tools (e.g., MERINO 1994). In the beginning this was based on the index fossil approach and later on the identification of the internal homogeneity of lithic assemblages within which the different types are represented in recurring proportional and previously fixed intervals.

The names used to identify the different types of tools (scraper, burins, knives, etc.) allow us to see how the

---

[1] This denomination includes a large number of mineral remains generated in the production of consumer goods. These goods may have a wide variety of functions, permitting a human group to produce and maintain the conditions that permit their biological and social reproduction due to their participation:
- As products related to subsistence, both as construction materials by being part of walls, windbreaks, paved areas, fireplaces, etc. and as heat accumulators and diffusers, or as containers, among other uses.
- As products related to social identification: adornments, insignias, images, etc.
- As tools that unlike those mentioned above, permit the production of new consumer goods through the transformation of raw materials of all kinds. In this paper, we will deal with the latter.

hypothesis of use based on shape made an unjustified leap of inference to become a categorical statement of fact. The use of ethnographical analogies played a leading role in the creation of this nomenclature. Scholarly opinion happily moved from the formal comparison of archaeological lithic remains and their use by societies that utilised stone tools to the identification of functionality through the assimilation of their shape. The next inferential step was the association of current socio-economic models with those of prehistory.

Having said that, there were alternative proposals regarding the study of the function of lithic tools such as that put forward by the Soviet researcher S.A. Semenov from the perspective of historical materialism (SEMENOV 1957). This approach was either not taken seriously in the West as it clashed with the dominant academic theory, or devalued by considering the function of tools as just one more detail to be added to the existing typological lists.

ETHNOGRAPHICAL ANALOGIES

As we have mentioned above, ethnology was used as a justification and analogy as an instrument to propose a paradigm in order to recognise cultures for prehistory. But these affirmations went far beyond everything that ethnology and anthropology identified as defining traits of a culture. They even contradicted what is normally considered to be cultural.

From an ethnological point of view, we will see that a human group is never defined or characterised by the technological development that it achieves, let alone by the sum of the morphologies of their tools. What defines the identity of a human group is its specific social organisation for production and reproduction, which is the result of its historic development. Specific strategies for biological and social reproduction present at a given moment are what allow us to describe a group and differentiate it from others, whether they are contemporary or not. The concept of organisational strategy refers to the execution of an articulated and planned series of processes (established, regulated and determined socially) that govern the productive and reproductive activities of societies (TERRADAS 1998; 2001). As its name indicates, the term we have used to describe this concept implicitly includes strategic (its objective is the achievement of a goal) and organisational (its planning and execution is indicative of an organised structure) qualities.

It is in this context, and more specifically within the area of organisational strategies that affect the management of mineral resources, that the production of lithic tools should be understood as an intermediate element; a medium by which to carry out a series of necessary tasks within the strategies mentioned above, and it can never be interpreted as an end in itself. Technology is, therefore, the material expression (as far as the development of work processes is concerned) of the hierarchically ordered strategies of production and reproduction implemented by the social group. It is from this perspective that the study of lithic remains reveals all its interest and inferential potential: in the understanding of how and why the specific strategies of the production process have been designed and developed, and in the identification of their material manifestations, which are an indispensable element in order to be able to describe both the social character of the group and its historical development.

In this framework, neither ethnology nor anthropology was able to provide answers about how to approach the study of lithic remains in archaeology. Their artificial and extreme division into two disciplines depending on the different objects of study, forgetting that they shared the same final objective, made it difficult to achieve the synthesis that could have helped to overcome the problem. Consequently, ethnological and anthropological monographies are used as a basis from which to make direct analogies. This mechanism is limited to showing the plausibility of the hypothesis made by the archaeologist by finding a real case in some anthropological document, which proves the hypothetical proposal. In this way great inferential leaps continue to be made that lead to a situation in which, with the same accurately studied data, such different interpretations are made that they may even be contradictory.

INSTRUMENTAL ETHNOARCHAEOLOGY

During the 1960s the axiom that archaeology (understood to be the scholarly study of preterite material remains) was unable to explain the social aspects arising from the remains that it discovered because social organisation did not itself leave any material remains. As a result, ethnology was increasingly used to provide interpretations in prehistoric archaeology; but this time the shortcomings of ethnology were to be resolved.

The proposal was to take an archaeological look at ethnographical societies; in other words, to take into account the material aspects and results of the way humans behave in their daily lives. This is would be known as ethnoarchaeology. It was not yet a sub-discipline, but under this title different approaches and practices were put forward which received names such as *active archaeology*, *living archaeology*, *ethnographic archaeology*, among others. It was not until the end of the 1970s that the name ethnoarchaeology gained general acceptance, above all within the so-called new archaeology and middle-range theories (BINFORD 1972; 1978; 1983). In this way, the study of present-day primitive peoples was developed in order to have analogies that could be useful to understand the way of life in prehistoric times, although this did not imply the discovery of global explanations for the processes of change that these prehistoric societies had undergone.

Having said that, the concept of ethnoarchaeology can be interpreted in different ways. Perhaps the only feature that they have in common is the establishment of some kind of link between archaeology, ethnology and cultural anthropology. All these disciplines succeeded in making the use of ethnographic analogy more sophisticated and better. At the same time, it showed the flaws in many archaeological practices while improving methods for recovering remains and generating data. However, they did not succeed in improving the explanations originating from archaeology. In other words, not a single genuine change took place that would allow it to enlarge its scope as a science, while continuing to generate ethnographical analogies (albeit more rigorous ones) for the study of prehistoric societies.

Also within this context, but from archaeological research, there emerged the so-called *paleoethnography* or *French prehistoric ethnology* (KARLIN et al. 1992), whose most significant representative is A. Leroi-Gourhan (1964; 1965). Along with J. Tixier, this author formulated in the 1960s the concept of *chaîne opératoire* as a research tool to be used in the study of the production of stone tools. This concept was a development of the study of technical processes carried out during the 1950s by French cultural anthropologists like M. Mauss and M. Maget, and is widely known and used in European prehistoric archaeology, being present in the vast majority of work on lithic tools (for example, in Spain: MORA et al. 1992). These works adopt the practical categories established by the *chaîne opératoire*, while omitting the implicit theoretical assumptions (PIE & VILA 1992).

ETHNOARCHAEOLOGY IN ARCHAEOLOGY

One important fact was missing from all these proposals which emerged during the 1960s, and it is that ethnoarchaeology allows one to work in archaeology without using ethnographical analogies. Our ethnoarchaeological proposal involves, first of all, understanding it as a resource with which it is possible to contrast archaeological methodologies. In other words, to contrast the validity of the methodology with the plausibility of the information which is supplied (ESTEVEZ & VILA 1998). We need to check that archaeology itself, with the methods and techniques that it is developing nowadays, is able to answer the questions about social dynamics (ARGELES et al. 1995; ESTEVEZ et al. 1998; RUIZ & BRIZ 1998; VILA & RUIZ 2001) and, if this is so, evaluate this explanatory potential and the limits of its application. In this way, we aim to evaluate the possibility of obtaining truthful knowledge about the origins of human societies, their internal dynamics and their historical development. With the results from this contrastive analysis, we will be in a position to discover the shortcomings of current archaeological methodology and we will know what approach to use in order to correct them.

Ethnoarchaeology, therefore, as we see it, should put archaeological methodology to the test in order to achieve an appropriate methodological framework for the study of the socio-economic dynamics of prehistoric societies (ESTEVEZ & VILA 1995b; 1998; VILA & PIANA 1993). This contrastive analysis would have an impact on everything for the very notion of archaeological record to the methods and techniques used in their recovery, including its epistemological foundations, and would be carried through the dialectical contradiction between the different types of sources, within a system of hierarchically organised terms (VILA & ESTEVEZ 2001).

We can currently state that the theoretical and conceptual framework of normative archaeology is not useful for describing social organisation properly. In relation to the issue that we are dealing with here, groups of lithic remains, in order to affirm this uselessness we could take as a starting point the lack of any link between the typological classifications used and the social dynamics of production of the past. The typological proposals are a classificatory system, not a means of interpretation. On the other hand, ethnoarchaeology, as we have described it above, shows us that these remains can give us relevant social information if we make use of suitable categories and significant and adequate associations. Although it has not been developed exclusively for the study of stone tools, ethnoarchaeology should allow us to see the most valid variables in the study of lithic remains, depending on how much they contribute to the general objective we are pursuing.

In the course of the ethnoarchaeological projects we are working on in Tierra del Fuego, Argentina (ESTEVEZ & VILA 1995a; 1998; PIANA et al. 1992; VILA et al. 1998) we have carried out archaeological excavations at a number of different settlements: *Tunel VII*, *Lanashuaia* and *Alashawaia*, all of which were occupied several times when the indigenous societies came into contact with the new European settlers. These sites are located on the northern coast of the Beagle Channel (Figure 1), although they are situated in different environments and may present regional differences of a quantitative nature due to the availability of natural resources. Thanks to the large amount of ethnohistorical information available, we know that these places were occupied by the same group of hunter-gatherers called the *Yamana* by ethnographers. This information, of a widely varied nature and significance, is what allows us to answer certain questions that we wished to pose from the perspective of prehistoric archaeology.

The study of these archaeological remains has allowed us to confirm the uselessness of formal and technological categories for an interpretation from the perspective of social archaeology (CLEMENTE 1997; CLEMENTE & TERRADAS 1993; CLEMENTE et al. 1996; MANSUR & VILA 1993; TERRADAS 1997; 2001; TERRADAS et al. 1999). These categories not only fail to contribute to knowledge about production, they also isolate tools from the social context that generated them and which give them meaning. It is very clear that they are not suitable for describing groups.

If we were to study the lithic remains of these sites using the parameters of the classical typologies, we would separate them culturally according to: typological level, proportions of raw materials, methods and techniques of manufacture, and the relative uses that they represent. This shows the unsuitability of the parameters of historical-cultural archaeology to classify human groups according to lithic typologies. This should tell us that what defines a social group is something much wider. It is obvious that if we wish to extract information from these sources, we

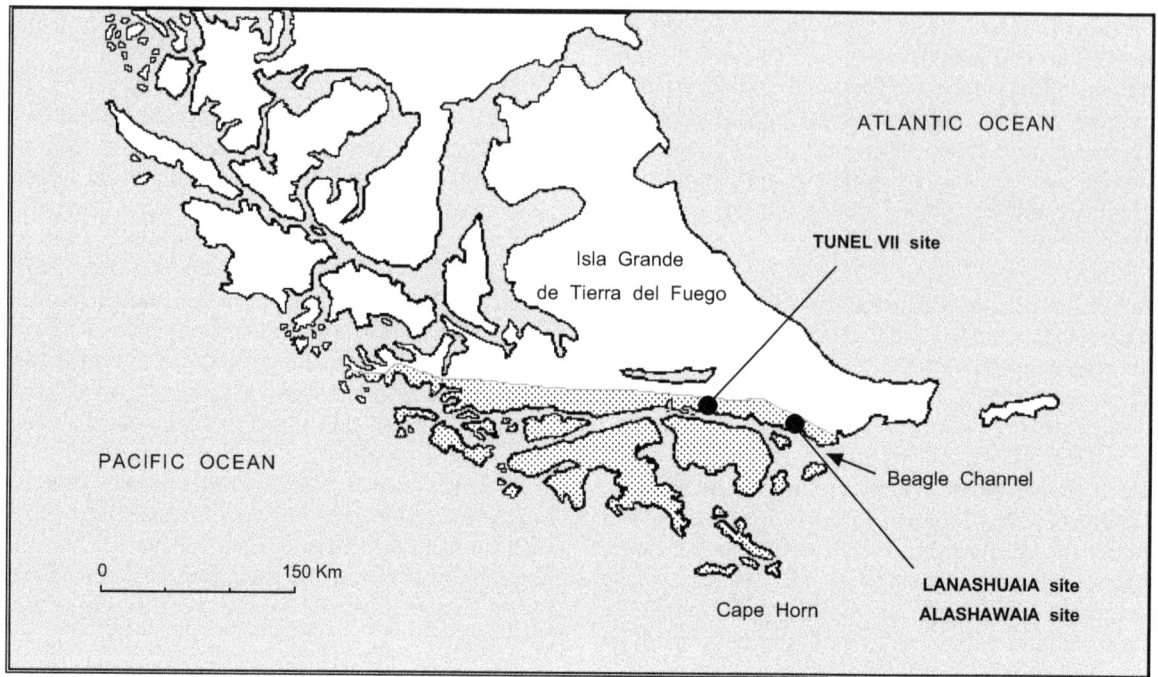

Figure 1: Geographical map of the Tierra del Fuego archipelago (Argentina-Chile) with the distribution of *Yamana* people (shaded area) and the location of archaeological sites mentioned on the text

must develop suitable methodologies that provide us with reliable information. This information should link up with other elements that make up archaeological record.

CATEGORIES OF ANALYSIS

The study of lithic remains should match with archaeological knowledge of the social dynamics of global production and reproduction. Consequently, we need radically different categories to those which are normally used, as well as a different hierarchical order for them as well.

We know that lithic remains recovered from a socially significant unit of observation (occupation floor, layer) are the result of either work processes related to the manufacture of stone tools, or of the use of the latter in other processes linked to the production of new consumer goods. Taking this fact as a starting point, the element on which we construct the hierarchical order of our study proposal is the identification of the stone tools, which is the main objective of the lithic production process. This is why we need prior identification of those lithic remains that have been used in later productive activities, which we will refer to as **tools**. Theses tools permit the production of new consumer goods through the transformation of raw materials of all kinds. This permits an increase in human productive capacity by raising the energy level of a person's labour beyond his or her physiological limitations (LUMBRERAS 1981). The importance of their study comes from the possibilities that this offers to evaluate what level has been achieved in the development of the productive forces of a society, as well as the possibility to reconstruct the basis of its economic system, as they are its legacy (KOROBKOVA 1983).

On the archaeological level, tools can be recognised by means of the micro- and macroscopic alterations to their edges, ridges and surfaces, which are the result of their use on different types of material. Consequently, functional analysis is essential in order to identify tools and their role in the production process.

In the development of the lithic production process, and as a result of the manufacture of the desired products (tools), a waste number of products are derived. We shall divide these into rejects and by-products. A **reject** or rejected element is something that is surplus to the process of production and use of tools, which is voluntarily discarded. A **by-product** is something that is produced involuntarily during the creation of the desired product. These concepts will be defined by the objectives that drive lithic production and its use in each case (Figure 2).

As far as its archaeological recognition is concerned, a reject displays morphotechnical and morphometric characteristics that are very similar to those displayed by tools. The key element to distinguish between the two categories is some sign that the tools have been used in other activities that were productive. Rejects, despite their similarity to tools, were for some reason not integrated into other work processes. By-products can be identified by the fact that they display no sign of having been used nor bear any morphotechnical or morphometric resemblance to the other categories mentioned above. In optimal situations and depending on the time when these by-products were generated, it is possible to distinguish between production by-products (for example, a flake derived from the preparation of a striking platform, or a microflake obtained by retouch), and by-products of use (for example, those minute remains of the tool that have been chipped off during use).

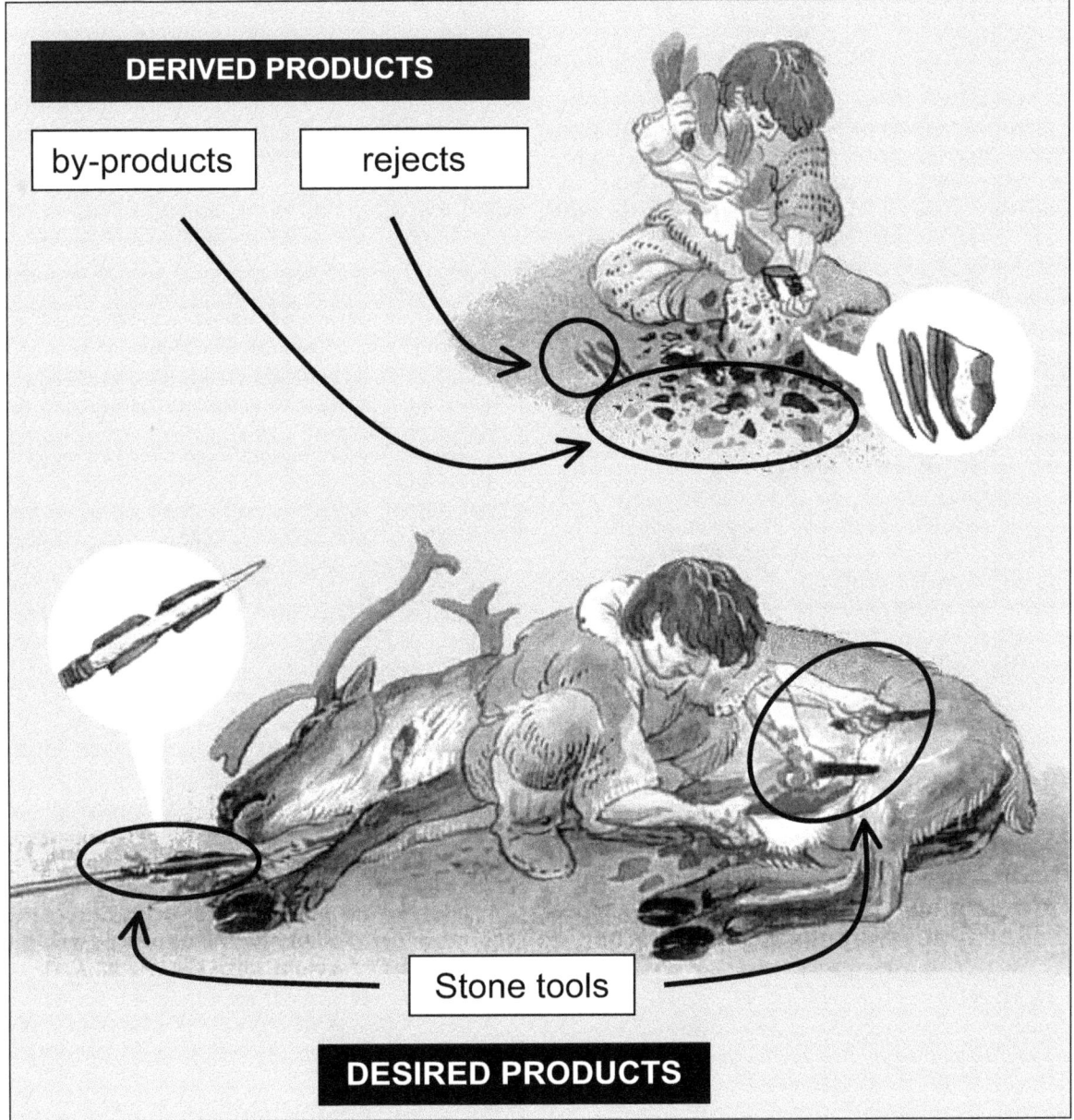

Figure 2: Simulated example with the proposed categories of analysis
(elaborated by authors based on a drawing published by KARLIN et al. 1992)

The relevance of these categories is due to their usefulness, as they allow us to determine the objectives of production. In other words, they allow us to discover what products were in demand or, put another way, what consumer goods it was necessary to produce at a given time (specific utensils), as well as the needs that had to be addressed (specific use). In this way, we will be able to reconstruct and describe the strategies designed and carried out in the management of mineral resources for the production of lithic tools and other consumer goods. This is possible by studying the interaction of the different elements of production, which will give us access to a dynamic and economic dimension of the development of these strategies and their material results.

The development of these strategies involves the linking of different production processes, which cause constant and progressive alterations in the raw material. This provokes a series of changes in its original properties and conditions in relation to both their spatial context and their volumetric and morphological characteristics. These alterations begin in the geological context from which the raw material was extracted in order to be incorporated into a socio-economic dynamic, and ends in the archaeological contexts from which the resulting effects of its transformation and use have been recovered.

At the same time, knowledge of the nature and availability of the different mineral resources which were available to the societies included in the study, should permit us to discover which likely alternative strategies to those that have already been archaeologically documented. The usefulness and profitability of the latter, in relation to the nature and availability of mineral resources, are elements that should allow us to obtain an idea about the degree of technological development achieved by the societies included in the study.

The other categories relating to the social relations between men and women who produce, and as social agents, benefit from the results of production, are not to be found in the lithic remains themselves but, as ethnoarchaeology shows us, from an analysis of the area where these relations took place. As a physical space transformed by productive activities, the social space is considered to be a relevant analytical category, due to the fact that through its study it is possible to obtain information about the interaction between different social agents and collectives depending on the kind of activities that were linked to production, distribution and consumption (WÜNSCH 1995). It is equally possible to identify the basic tendencies that govern the resulting logistical strategies, based on the conditioning and cleaning of the area transformed by the social activity. In order to achieve this, we establish the premise that the spatial link between the elements of the archaeological record reflects the whole group of activities carried out. For their study it is necessary to design a methodology, which is closely linked to the analysis of the empirical record and based on the application of qualitative methods.

Authors' addresses

Ivan BRIZ
Consejo Superior de Investigaciones Científicas (CSIC)
Laboratory of Archaeology – Inst. «Milà i Fontanals»
Egipcíaques, 15. 08001 Barcelona? SPAIN
e-mail: ibriz@bicat.csic.es

Ignacio CLEMENTE
Consejo Superior de Investigaciones Científicas (CSIC)
Laboratory of Archaeology – Inst. «Milà i Fontanals»
Egipcíaques, 15. 08001 Barcelona, SPAIN
e-mail: ignacio@bicat.csic.es

Jordi PIJOAN
Universitat Autònoma de Barcelona
Departament d'Antropologia Social i Prehistòria
Facultat de Lletres - Edifici B. 08193 Bellaterra, SPAIN
e-mail: jordi.pijoan@uab.es

Xavier TERRADAS
Consejo Superior de Investigaciones Científicas (CSIC)
Laboratory of Archaeology – Inst. «Milà i Fontanals»
Egipcíaques, 15. 08001 BARCELONA (Spain)
e-mail: terradas@bicat.csic.es

Assumpció VILA
Consejo Superior de Investigaciones Científicas (CSIC)
Laboratory of Archaeology – Inst. «Milà i Fontanals»
Egipcíaques, 15. 08001 Barcelona, SPAIN
e-mail: avila@bicat.csic.es

Bibliography

ARGELÉS, T., BONET, A., CLEMENTE, I., ESTÉVEZ, J., GIBAJA, J., LUMBRERAS, L.G., PIQUÉ, R., RÍOS, M., TAULÉ, M.A., TERRADAS, X., VILA, A. & WÜNSCH, G., 1995, Teoría para una praxis. «Splendor realitatis». In *1º Congresso de Arqueologia peninsular. Trabalhos de Antropologia e Etnologia* 35 (1), p. 501-507.

BINFORD, L.R., 1972, *An archaeological perspective*. New York: Seminar Press.

BINFORD, L.R., 1978, *Nunamiut Ethnoarchaeology*. New York: Academic Press.

BINFORD, L.R., 1983, *In pursuit of the past. Decoding the archaeological record*. London: Thames & Hudson.

CLEMENTE, I., 1997, *Los instrumentos líticos de Túnel VII: una aproximación etnoarqueológica (Treballs d'Etnoarqueologia 2)*. Madrid: Universitat Autònoma de Barcelona & Consejo Superior de Investigaciones Científicas.

CLEMENTE, I. & TERRADAS, X., 1993, Matières premières et fonctions: l'exemple de l'outillage lithique des *Yamana*. In *Traces et fonctions: les gestes retrouvés (E.R.A.U.L. 50)*, directed by P.C. Anderson et alii. Liège: Université de Liège, p. 513-521.

CLEMENTE, I., MANSUR, M.E., TERRADAS, X. & VILA, A., 1996, Al César lo que es del César... o los instrumentos líticos como instrumentos de trabajo. In *Arqueología: sólo Patagonia (Ponencias de las 2as Jornadas de Arqueología de la Patagonia)*, edited by J. Gómez Otero. Puerto Madryn (Argentina): Consejo Nacional de Investigaciones Científicas y Técnicas, p. 319-331.

ESTÉVEZ, J. & VILA, A., 1995a (coords.), *Encuentros en los conchales fueguinos (Treballs d'Etnoarqueologia 1)*. Barcelona: Universitat Autònoma de Barcelona & Consejo Superior de Investigaciones Científicas.

ESTÉVEZ, J. & VILA, A., 1995b, Etnoarqueología: el nombre de la cosa. In *Encuentros en los conchales fueguinos (Treballs d'Etnoarqueologia 1)*, coordinated by J. Estévez & A. Vila. Barcelona: Universitat Autònoma de Barcelona & Consejo Superior de Investigaciones Científicas, p. 17-23.

ESTÉVEZ, J. & VILA, A., 1998, Tierra del Fuego, lugar de encuentros. *Revista de Arqueología americana* 15, p. 187-219.

ESTÉVEZ, J., VILA, A., TERRADAS, X., PIQUÉ, R., TAULÉ, M., GIBAJA, J. & RUIZ, G., 1998, Cazar o no cazar, ¿es ésta la cuestión?. *Boletín de Antropología americana* 33, p. 5-24.

KARLIN, C., PIGEOT, N. & PLOUX, S., 1992, L'Ethnologie préhistorique. *La Recherche* 247 (23), p. 1106-1116.

KOROBKOVA, G.F., 1983, Development of the productive forces and of working tools as a prerequisite of the evolution of new types of economy. *Journal of Central Asia* VI (1), p. 73-80.

LEROI-GOURHAN, A., 1964, *Le geste et la parole, I: Technique et langage*. Paris: Albin Michel.

LEROI-GOURHAN, A., 1965, *Le geste et la parole, II: La mémoire et les rythmes*. Paris: Albin Michel.

LUMBRERAS, L.G., 1981, *La Arqueología como ciencia social*. Lima: Ediciones Peisa.

MANSUR, M.E. & VILA, A., 1993, L'analyse du matériel lithique dans la caractérisation archéologique d'une unité sociale. In *Traces et fonctions: les gestes retrouvés (E.R.A.U.L. 50)*, directed by P.C. Anderson et alii. Liège: Université de Liège, p. 501-512.

MERINO, J.M., 1994, *Tipología lítica (Munibe Antropología /Arkeologia 9)*. Donostia: Aranzadi Zientzi Elkartea.

MORA, R., TERRADAS, X., PARPAL, A. & PLANA, C., 1992 (eds.), *Tecnología y cadenas operativas líticas (Treballs d'Arqueologia 1)*. Barcelona: Universitat Autònoma de Barcelona.

PIANA, E.L., VILA, A., ORQUERA, L.A. & ESTÉVEZ, J., 1992, Chronicles of «Ona-Ashaga»: Archaeology in the

Beagle Channel (Tierra del Fuego, Argentina). *Antiquity* 66, p. 771-783.

PIE, J. & VILA, A., 1992, Relaciones entre objetivos y métodos en el estudio de la industria lítica. In *Tecnología y cadenas operativas líticas (Treballs d'Arqueologia 1)*, edited by R. Mora *et alii*. Barcelona: Universitat Autònoma de Barcelona, p. 271-278.

RUIZ, G. & BRIZ, I., 1998, Re-pensando la re-producción. *Boletín de Antropología americana* 33, p. 79-90.

SEMENOV, S.A., 1957, *Pervobitnaya tejnika (Materiali y Isledovania po Arjeologuii SSSR 54)*. Moskva: Russian Academy of Sciences.

TERRADAS, X., 1997, Lithic raw material procurement strategies by the *Yamana* people (Tierra del Fuego, Argentina). In *Man and flint (Proceedings of the VIIth International Flint Symposium)*, edited by R. Schild & Z. Sulgostowska. Warszawa: Polish Academy of Sciences, p. 123-126.

TERRADAS, X., 1998, La gestión de los recursos minerales: propuesta teórico-metodológica para el estudio de la producción lítica en la Prehistoria. In *Actes de la 2a reunió de treball sobre aprovisionament de recursos lítics a la Prehistòria (Rubricatum 2)*, edited by J. Bosch *et alii*. Gavà (Barcelona): Museu de Gavà, p. 21-28.

TERRADAS, X., 2001, *La gestión de los recursos minerales en las sociedades cazadoras-recolectoras (Treballs d'Etnoarqueologia 4)*. Madrid: Consejo Superior de Investigaciones Científicas.

TERRADAS, X., VILA, A., CLEMENTE, I. & MANSUR, M.E., 1999, Ethno-neglect or the contradiction between ethnohistorical sources and the archaeological record. The case of stone tools of the *Yamana* people (Tierra del Fuego, Argentina). In *Ethno-analogy and the reconstruction of prehistoric artefact use and production (Urgeschichtliche Materialhefte Series 14)*, edited by L. Owen & M. Porr. Tübingen: Mo Vince Verlag, p. 103-115.

VILA, A. & ESTÉVEZ, J., 2001, Calibrando el método: Arqueología en Tierra del Fuego. *Astigi Vetus (Revista del Museo Histórico Municipal de Écija)* 1, p. 63-72.

VILA, A. & PIANA, E.L., 1993, Arguments per a una Etnoarqueologia. *Revista d'Etnologia de Catalunya* 3. p 151-154.

VILA, A. & RUIZ, G., 2001, Información etnológica y el análisis de la reproducción social. El caso *Yamana*. *Revista Española de Antropología Americana* 31, p. 275-291.

VILA, A., ESTÉVEZ, J., ÁLVAREZ, A. & PIANA, E.L., 1998, *Marine resources at the Beagle Channel prior to the industrial exploitation: an archaeological evaluation (Final Repport to Directorate General XII of the European Commission)*. Bruxelles.

WÜNSCH, G., 1995, De la articulación espacial del registro arqueológico a la gestión del espacio social: Un ejemplo de aplicación del análisis de las interrelaciones espaciales. In *Encuentros en los conchales fueguinos (Treballs d'Etnoarqueologia 1)*, coordinated by J. Estévez & A. Vila. Barcelona: Universitat Autònoma de Barcelona & Consejo Superior de Investigaciones Científicas, p. 127-142.

DEEP IMPACT: STONES IN BONES.
SOME THOUGHTS ABOUT THE ETHNOARCHAEOLOGY CONTRAST.
A VIEW FROM TIERRA DEL FUEGO (EXTREME SOUTH AMERICA)

Laura MAMELI, Jordi ESTEVEZ & Ernesto Luis PIANA

Abstract: The archaeological research in recent Yamana settlements on the northern coast of the Beagle Channel is contrasted against the ethnographic information. The analysis of traces left by stone tools and by weapons on bones demonstrates some biases concerning the written information as well as some unexpected hunting strategies. The conclusions extracted point to the necessity of a very careful macroscopic examination of lithic inclusions in bone material.

Résumé : La recherche archéologique sur les sites Yamana de la côte nord du Channel Beagle a été confrontée avec les informations ethnologiques. L'analyse des traces laisses sur la surface des os par des instruments et les armes en pierre ont démontrée quelques déviations de l'information écrite et la pratique de stratégies de chasse non prévues. Les conclusions nous portent à la nécessité de faire une inspection macroscopique rigoureuse des inclusions de pierre dans les surfaces des ossements.

INTRODUCTION

Archaeological research on the northern coast of the Beagle Channel in Tierra del Fuego since 1975 has provided a historical sequence from the first settlement on the islands until the 19th century, after European contact with the so-called *Yamana* people (Orquera & Piana, 1999 a).

As a result of two Argentinean and Spaniard research projects, we have analyzed the impact of European exploitation on the marine resources along with changes in environment over the last 6000 years[1]. Our goal was to evaluate the impact of massive industrial exploitation on the natives' resources and its influence on their catastrophic extinction as an organized society.

During this process, we compiled and extensively evaluated data from ethnographic and historical written sources (Orquera & Piana, 1999b), as well as ethnographic, graphic and photographic collections deposited in the main ethnographic museums in Europe (London, Paris, Rome, Madrid, Gøtteborg, Berlin, Wien and Saint Petersburg (Estévez & Vila 2001). Our first aim during the projects was to contrast the resulting ethnographic image with the archaeological record from some sites dating to the European contact period. In this process, we wanted to gain an objective image of the last moments of the people living on the northern coast of the Beagle Channel and, at the same time, to improve and test archaeological methods and inference systems (Piana, ea. 1992).

Our field work in two recent settlements (figure 1), Túnel VII and Lanashuaia, covered in both cases the whole surface occupied by a social unit (a hut and its surrounding working area) obtaining therefore a complete set of residues, result of the production and consumption activities done at these places (Estévez & Vila eds. 1995; Piana, ea. 1999). We focused the main effort of our studies on archaeozoological materials (Estévez, 1995, Estévez, ea. 1995; Estévez & Martínez 1998; Estévez, ea. 2001; Juan Muns, 1992; Juan Muns, 1994; Mameli, 2000). As part of our objectives, we stressed the analysis of the faunal record as far as possible trying to develop methods to squeeze the information we can obtain from (Estévez, 1995). A strong correlated study of the whole archaeological information, experimental replications and the analysis of the ancient ecosystem, could offer a quite good image of the systems for obtaining, processing and the distribution of animal resources, as well as the evaluation of the weight in the economy of every animal class. At a first glance the image matches quite well with the overall ethnographic information (Estévez, ea. 1995). Nevertheless some striking and contrasting points arose, especially as we risen the standards of analysis to a higher level, going beyond the simple record of the relative frequency of taxa and elements to the refitting, re-articulation, macroscopic analysis (from 10 to 80x magnification) of icneology on all bones surfaces together with distribution analysis for determining the destination of body parts as well as deposition dynamics and relating this information with the analysis of the production and the use -through usewear analysis- of lithic and bone tools (Terradas ea. 1999; Clemente, 1997 and Piana & Estévez, 1995). Therefore this contrast, at its turn, sets the question back to the standards of archaeozoological work normally used. In that way, analyzing the consequences of this close encounter between Ethnography and Archaeology we try to increase our knowledge about the last Yamana and at the same time to improve and verify the archaeological (in this case the archaeozoological) methods.

---

[1] "Archeological Contrast of the ethnographic Image of the Magellan - Fuegian Canoers in the Nortern Coast of the Beagle Channel" between 1987-1994, was a joint project of the Argentinian and Spanish Research Councils (Vila & Estévez eds., 1995) and "Marine Resources at the Beagle Channel Region prior to the Industrial Explotation: An Archaeological Evaluation" was an European Union Joint research project (1994-1998) coordinated from CSIC-Barcelona.

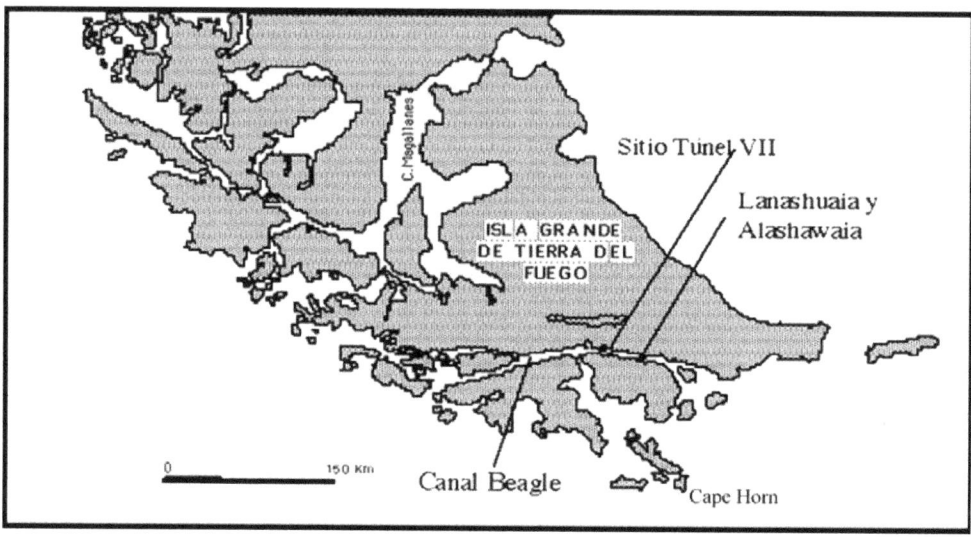

Figure 1. Map of Tierra del Fuego islands and location of the sites studied.

THE EXPLOITATION SYSTEM AFTER THE ETHNOGRAPHIC SOURCES

Animal exploitation strategies by *Yamana* people were described in detail by ethnographic sources (Orquera y Piana, 1999b). Ethnographic hunting implements are well represented too in the collections of European ethnographic museums. All written and graphic information of Tierra del Fuego canoe Indians draw them as people heavily oriented to coastal resources exploitation, based in collecting mussels, fishing, capturing birds and using harpoons from canoes to hunt sea lions. Since 1624, the drawings by the Nassau Fleet (reported by J.l'Hermite), people are shown using these weapons as well as bows and arrows (figure 2). But the temporary large span of the information sets some problems. A series of contradictions between the different authors arose. It is sometimes possible to resolve some of them analyzing critically every ethnographic source. Some times the bias on the same source or the time span and the development of the extractive practices by Yamana people can be explained. It is possible for instance to notice a change between the chronicles before and after 1869. The frequency of sea lion hunting activities seems to decrease probably due to the overhunting of these animals by Euroamerican fur-hunter ships.

The strong parallel between the first pictures of men with harpoons in the 17th century (in the work of Sebald de Weert, 1646) and the last pictures token at the end of the 19th by the Mission Scientifique du Cap Horn (Figure 3) demonstrates another bias. There is a continuity in the interest to describe and underline specially men's hunting activities. All writers resume the use -from canoes or on land- of harpoons for hunting of sea lions, otters or sometimes to kill larger animals (such as dolphins or whales).

This weapon has a -single or double toggled- detachable bone point. There are some whole harpoons and many harpoon points. Table 1 compiles the measurements of those noted as "Yamana" and the histogram in figure 4 shows a tendency to a normal length around 26 cm. But there are some exemplars longer than 55 cm. In its ethnographic description Gusinde describes in 1937 (pages 460 and 501-503) that people employed harpoon-points longer than 40 cm to kill larger prey such as whales.

The harpoon with detachable or toggling point was the most adequate one for hunting pinniped and the use perfectly fitted the hunting on the sea and canoe use for searching and capture.

There are other differences between the earlier and the later sources. The first drawings clearly show the use of bows and arrows whereas after the ethnographic written sources from second half of the 19th. Century (since Lovisato 1883 page 7) their use is not so often mentioned and to beginnings of the XXth Century it is said arrow points were no more manufactured and acquired only through changes with their neighbors Selk'nam of the North. Yamana bows where collected by the Mission Scientifique du Cap Horn in 1883 but are described to bee

Figure 2. First drawing of Fueguian canoe people showing their weapons.

Figure 3. Picture of Yamana using harpoons: in the 19th century (left) and in the 17th century.

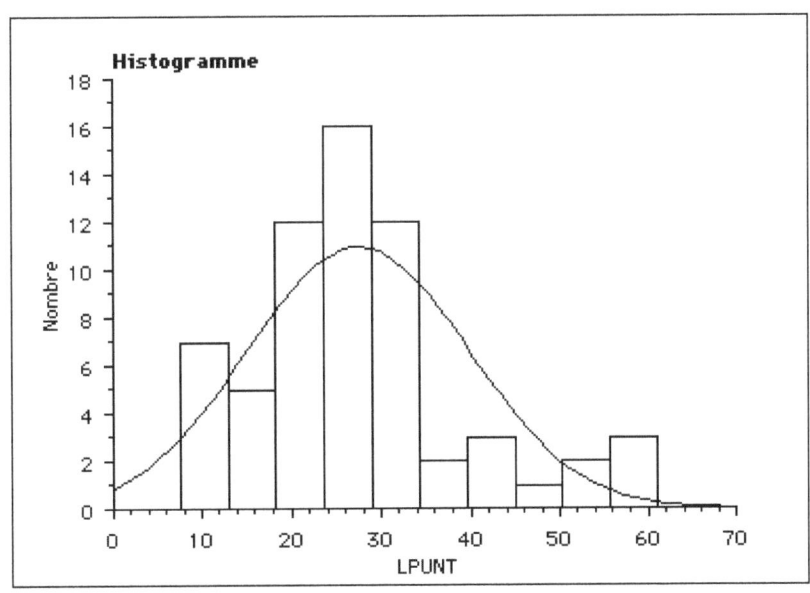

Figure 4. Variability of harpoon length in Yamana ethnographic collections.

less strong or efficient than the ones of the northern groups and only seldom used by these human groups to shot birds or guanaco.

We have analyzed 46 bows from Tierra del Fuego in Ethnographic collections. Some bows and arrows are refereed to Yamana people (one in London, three in Paris), but there are also some others (one in London, three in the Vatican, Wien and Berlin and two in Saint Petersburg) that can be attributed to canoe people (some very probably Yamana). There are some tendencies (without statistical significance) to a twofold model it cannot be specifically centered on one or another ethnic group. Most bows are longer than 140 cm but there are others around 124 cm and lastly one no longer than 78 cm. Those bows brought by the French scientific Mission –the ones with most guaranties of exact provenance show this flexibility of the models used by Yamana people.

Table 1. Statistic of harpoons in ethnographic collections.

Harpoon sizes	Max. length	Max. deep	Tooth length	Max. width	Basis length	Point width	Shaft width	Basis width
Mean value	29,9	1,4	18,9	2,9	9,4	4,3	1,8	2,9
Standard dev.	9,9	0,4	8,8	0,6	2,8	0,9	0,4	0,6
variability	1,1	0,0	1,0	0,1	0,5	0,1	0,0	0,1
variance	98,8	0,2	76,9	0,4	7,7	0,7	0,2	0,3
coef. variability	0,3	0,3	0,5	0,2	0,3	0,2	0,2	0,2
minimal	15,4	0,6	7,5	1,6	3,5	2,3	1,0	1,5
maximal	61,0	2,4	49,5	4,4	15,4	8,1	2,7	4,2
Variability	45,6	1,8	42,0	2,8	11,9	5,8	1,7	2,7
N	85,0	80,0	82,0	80,0	35,0	68,0	73,0	79,0

Table 2. measurements of Yamana arrows in ethnographic collections.

Yamana arrows	Length	Shaft diameter	Point length	Point width
Mean	67,00	0,76	2,79	1,50
stand.dev.	3,49	0,10	0,51	0,14
stand. error	0,44	0,01	0,19	0,05
variance	12,18	0,01	0,26	0,02
variab.coef.	0,05	0,13	0,18	0,09
minimal	57,50	0,60	2,20	1,20
maximal	84,00	1,00	3,70	1,60
variability	26,50	0,40	1,50	0,40
N.	64	51	7	8

Most of the points in ethnographic collections are made with European glass but there are still some done with lithic raw material. Despite the ethnographic sources there are some arrows noted Yamana included in the whole material with a larger ascription to Tierra del Fuego.

Within the same holder there is no arrowhead standardization, either in shape or in size. In an arrows group there are arrowheads of different shape, size and made on different raw materials (stone, glass and bone). On the other hand there is a certain uniformity in the shaft length. This is to be expectable because it is the most meaningful variable for its function. Surprisingly –and against what it was said by the recent Ethnography- the arrows classified as "*Yamana*" are not shorter than the classified as "Selk'nam": differences are not significant. Length measurements display a normal distribution. What may be observed is that the "Selk'nam" ones have a mean diameter (1.3 cm) thicker than the "*Yamana*" ones (0.7 cm). The arrow points have a very similar form (barbed and tangled triangle) to the points on the tip of the daggers but these are larger (mean of 5,6 cm length and 3 cm. width).

EXTRACTING ACTIVITIES AS SHOWN IN THE ARCHAEOLOGICAL RECORD

The archaeozoological work done in our research projects allowed a general overview of the subsistence's development since the first settlement on the island (Orquera & Piana, 1999a, Sciavinni, 1993, Estévez, ea. 2001) and a very detailed description of the extracting system in recent times (Estévez, ea. 1995; Estévez & Martínez, 1998).

The archaeological sites of European contact times on the northern coast of the Beagle Channel contained hunting implements, processing tools, as well parts of the prey (Orquera y Piana, 1999b; Clemente, 1997). In fact all the items documented in ethnographic collections that could be preserved in the archaeological record and almost all techniques employed in extracting these resources are present or can be induced by Archaeology (Vila & Estévez, 2000 and 2001).

Hunting of sea lions from canoes using harpoons are documented in the archaeological record: L.Orquera found

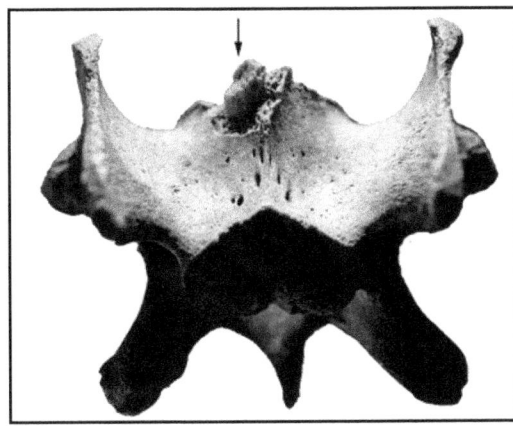

Figure 5. Sea lion cervical vertebra showing an embedded harpoon point.

Túnel VII site proves that a good deal of the lithic production process was stadial flaking, being one of the activities producing the highest quantity of residues (Clemente, 1997, Orquera & Piana, 1995 y Vila, ea. 1995, Terradas, ea. 1999) and oriented toward the production of bifacial elements. Within them, specially triangle arrowheads with barbs and tangle are equivalent in shape and measurements to the ethnographic ones (figure 6).

In Túnel VII within the occupational focus tens of thousands of lithic remains were found correlated to but six hundred pinniped remains (a maximum of 25 individuals) and roughly five thousand bird bones. At Lanashuaia 2019 three-dimensional registered lithic remains match 1158 bone remains. It turns evident that the lithic instrument making is a not negligible activity.

a cervical vertebra from a sea lion containing an embedded point of such a bone harpoon in the site Túnel I (figure 5) reflecting this capturing system, the most adequate to catch these animals. Nevertheless archaeological record shows some minor differences with the ethnographic information for harpoons. European ethnographic museums, for instance, lodge some very big harpoon points, up to 50 cm long, whereas in the archaeological record from our recent sites only some minor detachable points, no longer than 25 cm, have been found.

Archaeology enabled to discard Gusinde's assessment on the incapability of the Yamana for making bows and lithic arrowheads. On the contrary, lithic remains found i.e. at

BONES AND TOOLS: TRACES ON BONES

Both, instruments and the worked materials (including bones as part of prey's bodies), show traces of their close contacts. Actually, this is not a new issue in the archaeological research. From the beginnings of our discipline, scholars tried to recognize the use of stone implements and their traces on bones. The descriptions by H. Martin (1907) about traces of lithic instruments in bones from middle Paleolithic site of La Quina (in Europe) are a fine example. The paper about the flint points on an auroch from Denmark was a first direct proof of hunting techniques in the past (Hartz and Winge, 1906). The findings in 1926 in New Mexico of a Folsom point embedded in a Bison pelvis marked a landmark in the

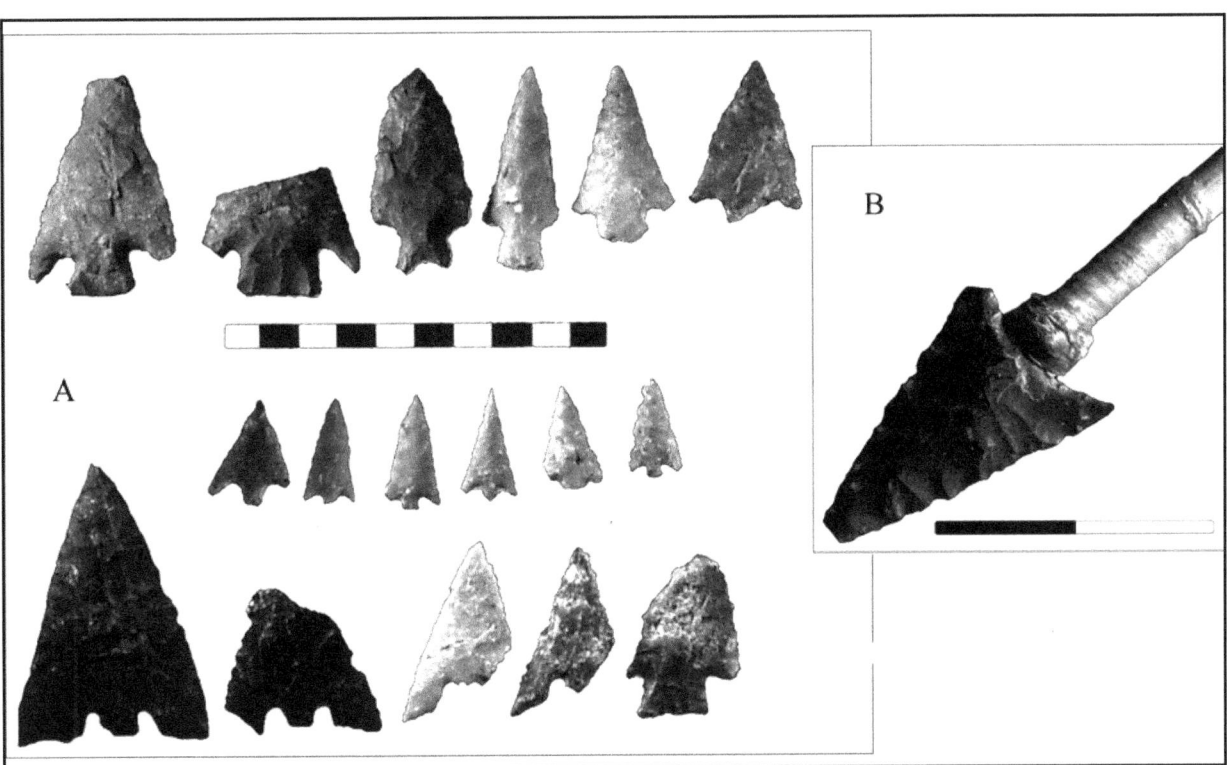

Figure 6. A) Archaeological bifacial points (arrow points in the center line, dagger points bottom line);
B) ethnographic arrow point.

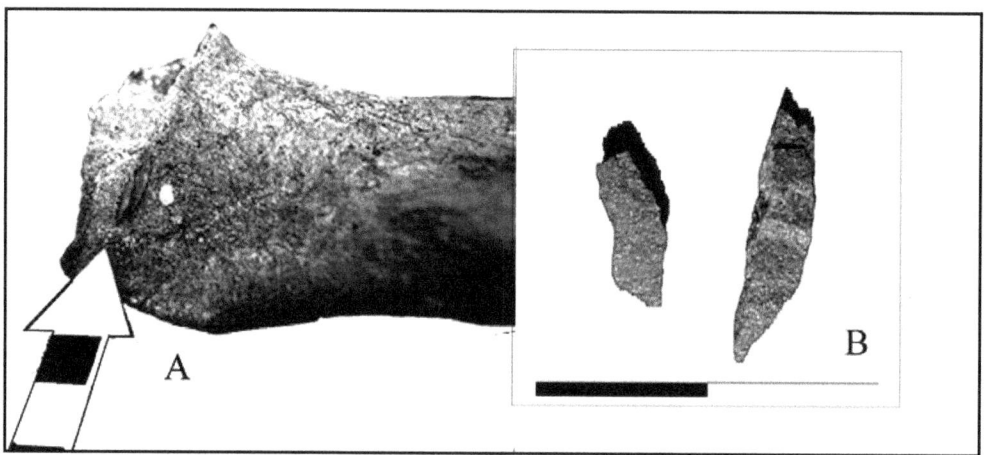

Figure 7. A) Minke whale rib with proximal end showing B) embedded stone chips.

history of the archaeology of America's first human settlement. Some years later, the descriptions of wounds on bones made by Noe-Nygaard (1974), allowed the description of hunting systems in the Mesolithic of Northern Europe.

Since the 1950s, Semenov's (Semenov 1981) work developing use-wear analysis offered the archaeologist the possibility to recognize directly the cinematic of lithic instruments and the sort of materials they worked on. Such approaches have become increasingly common, until now. Nevertheless, not so often a closer approach between the two types of information may be seen, and even less frequent is to have the possibility to contrast both of them with detailed information on a living system. As a result of our analysis, we found a very high percentage and intensity of working marks –butchering, cutting, slicing – on most bone surfaces of birds and pinnipedia.

Some of these marks denote a very heavy work on the animal carcasses. During the excavation of Lanashuaia (1995-1996) we were able to document directly the cutting up of a Minke whale by the chop-marks placed at the proximal end of its ribs found in the deposit base. Within these cut-marks we could observe (just at naked eye) the presence of small chips detached from the edge of a lithic tool. These micro flakes intruded in the bone while hard chopping (figure 7). Some remarkable chop marks placed on the vertebra's articulating surface of a killing whale from Túnel VII produced "piece of pie" like fragments of the *corpus vertebralis*.

In a first analysis of the remains belonging to those recent site's collections, we also found a proximal end of an ulna collapsed by the strike of a sharp object, producing a lenticular hole of 18.4 mm wide and 5.7 mm high (figure 8). Even though aware of it, at first it was not possible to attribute it to a concrete cause but, leaded by shape and size of the hole, we considered the possibility that it could be caused by the striking of an harpoon point as the ones documented in the site.

But most traces are very slight. That forced us to a closer look using macroscopic devices. During the macroscopic analysis of the Túnel VII bone collections, remains of a shell's edge were found embedded in the external side of a cormorant rib. These remains have to be product while processing the bird because they are inside anthropic cutting marks.

Finally the macroscopic analysis yielded a totally unexpected indication. It was an inlaying lithic small piece in the lateral left portion of a thoracic vertebra of a juvenile pinniped *(Artocephalus australis)* (Figure 9). This deep incrustation was not associated to any cut mark and displayed a lenticular section matching that of an arrowhead or a dagger point. This stone inclusion could only bee produced by a heavy stroke done by a tipped stone point but its reduced size (3,4 x 1,8 mm) and the not conclusive image of the X rays did not allow to specify nor to be sure about the tip of weapon. On the basis of the Ethnography the most probable way to cause this kind of injury was the use of dagger to kill sea lions on the mainland. The chop must be very heavy to embed the point to that deep. This moved us to review macroscopically all bones again to look closer to possible inclusions.

Meanwhile another thoracic vertebra of a young sea lion from a new site, Ajej (a rescue excavation no far from Ushuaia to the East dated from 1400 14C AP), that showed a big stone inclusion, could be examined. In this case there was no possible doubt: a very strong arrow stroke produced the penetration all-through the whole *corpus vertebralis* of a triangular-shaped arrow point identical to those found in the other mentioned recent sites. X ray analysis corroborated the naked eye inspection. The inlaying fragment with a perfect triangle shape and lenticular section measure 14.34 mm long, 7.9 mm wide and 2,65 mm of thickness (figure 10). The blow was heavy enough to traverse crashing the dorsal part of the bone, the point emerging at the *canalis vertebralis*. This piece leads to the certainty of the hunting of pinniped with bows and arrows. A hard arrow shot, that went into its belly, pierced the body and went trough the vertebra to the medullar channel, killed the sea lion. Both, arrow trajectory and the projectile penetration capability, lead to infer that the animal had being wounded on land while lying on a side (Piana ea. 2001).

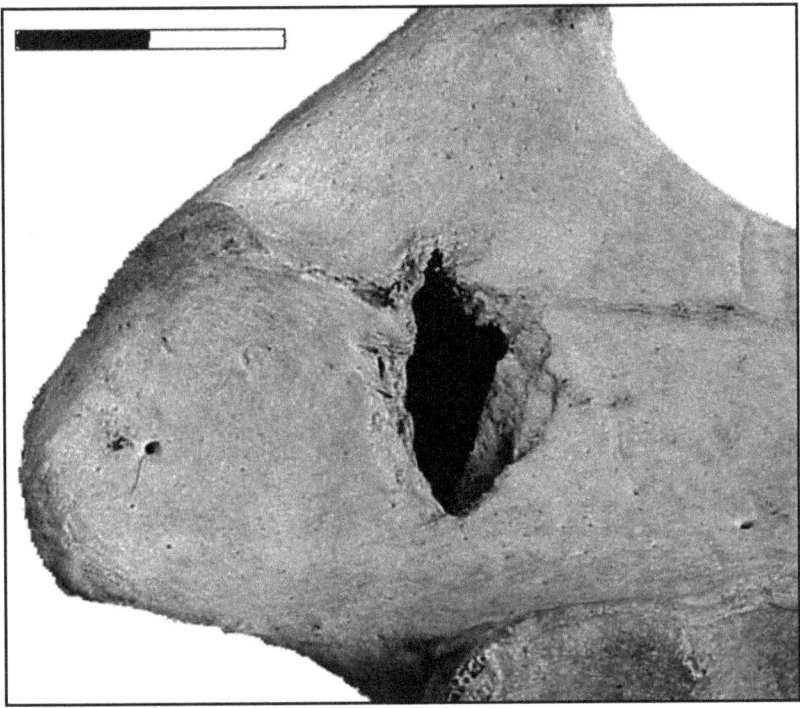

Figure 8. Sea lion proximal ulna with a lenticular hole.

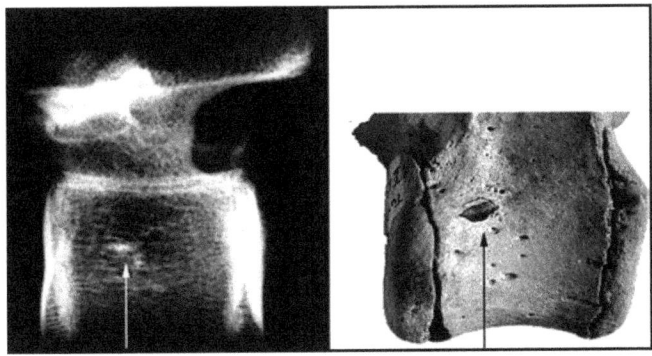

Figure 9- Sea lion thoracic vertebra showing embedded stone tip.

Finally, J.E. Moreno and A.Castro, researchers of the Museo de la Plata, kindly showed an equivalent case though from Cabo Blanco, coastal Patagonia. It is a guanaco (*Lama guanicoe*) vertebra with a hard arrow impact in the upper side portion of the corpus. The impact has to have being very strong because the inlaying arrowhead portion is in three pieces.

Taking such evidences into account, we conducted a new macroscopic inspection of all bone material of Túnel VII site, finding another much smaller inlaying lithic piece in the external portion of a sea lion rib.

Some traces, specially on ribs, were first interpreted as cut marks produced by slicing heavily a lithic knife on the side of the rib (figure 11) although clearly different from the more usual and normal cut, defleshing and slicing marks because their hardness, angle, location and isolation. They can be now better explained as the result of such arrow's impacts. During the reexamination of traces we observed some other lithic inclusions but associated to normal cut marks.

Leaded by the previously mentioned arrowhead imbedded in vertebras, and judging from the hole's size, shape and direction of the bone collapsing in the ulna described before, the wound is now regarded as a possible trace of an arrow shot. In short, there are evidences that in Tierra del Fuego pinniped were not only hunted in the way described by the ethnographic data but also, at least occasionally, with bows and arrows. Even though traces of this activity were previously seen, it was not until the Ajej findings that they could be regarded as traces of arrowhead impacts.

Still is to be supported that the majority of the pinniped hunting along the recent and ethnographic documented period had to be hunted in the sea, from canoes and with detachable points harpoons. Nevertheless, besides the hunting of females and puppies in occasional rookeries documented by age and sex profiles in the archaeozoological record (i.e., Túnel VII), other sea lions were opportunistic and occasionally hunted on land with different weapons. This turns meaningful while characterizing a general exploitation strategy of the prey resources: the ethnographic information leads to a normative way of hunting while the archaeological one proofs a more flexible behavior including opportunistic hunt by means not specialized for such a hunt. Actually, a sea lion hunting with bow and arrows from land is an activity with but few chances of success. It is not probable (and so is mentioned in the written sources) the existence of lasting rookeries within the maguellian-fueguian channels having the human predators easy access to them by canoes. Hypothetically, such rookeries would neither exist in pre European times (Schiavini 1993). More still, bows and arrows had fewer possibilities of successful hunting when compared with

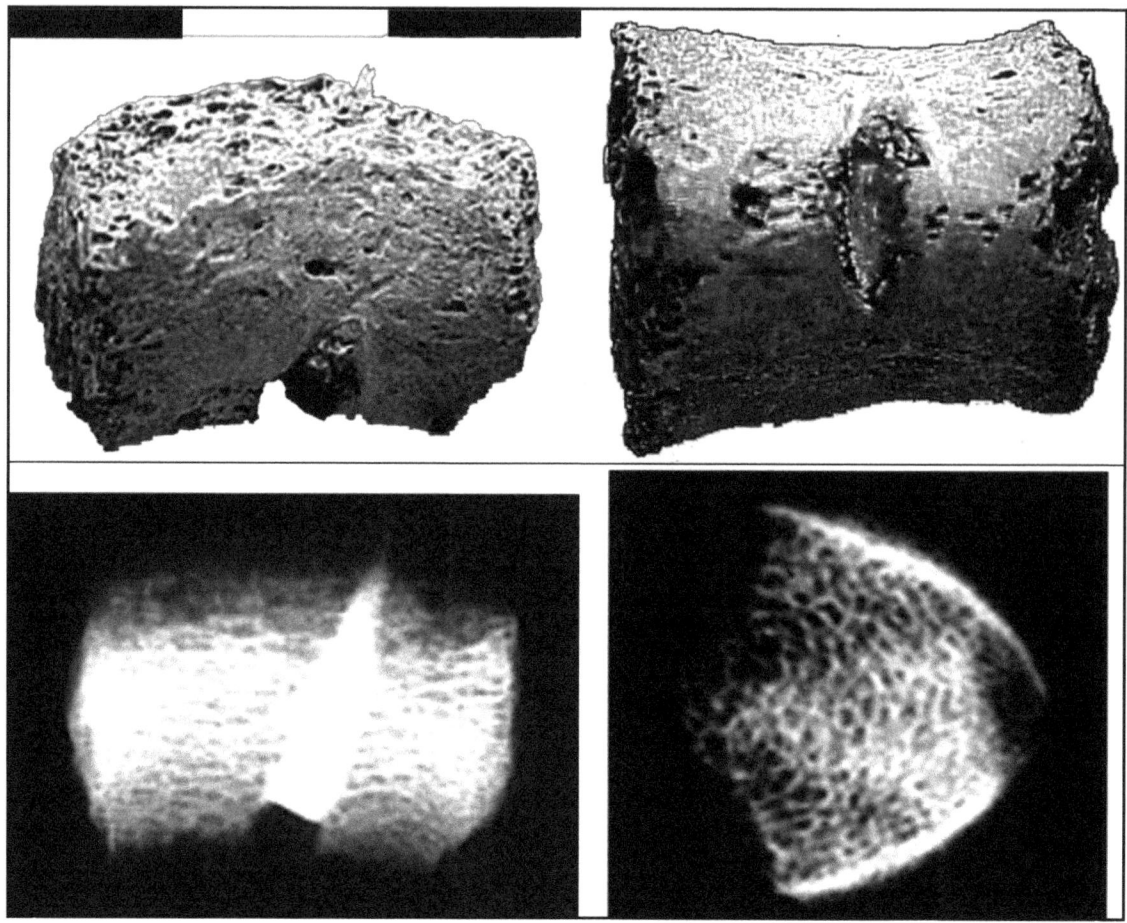

Figure 10. Sea lion vertebra from Ajej site with embedded arrow point.

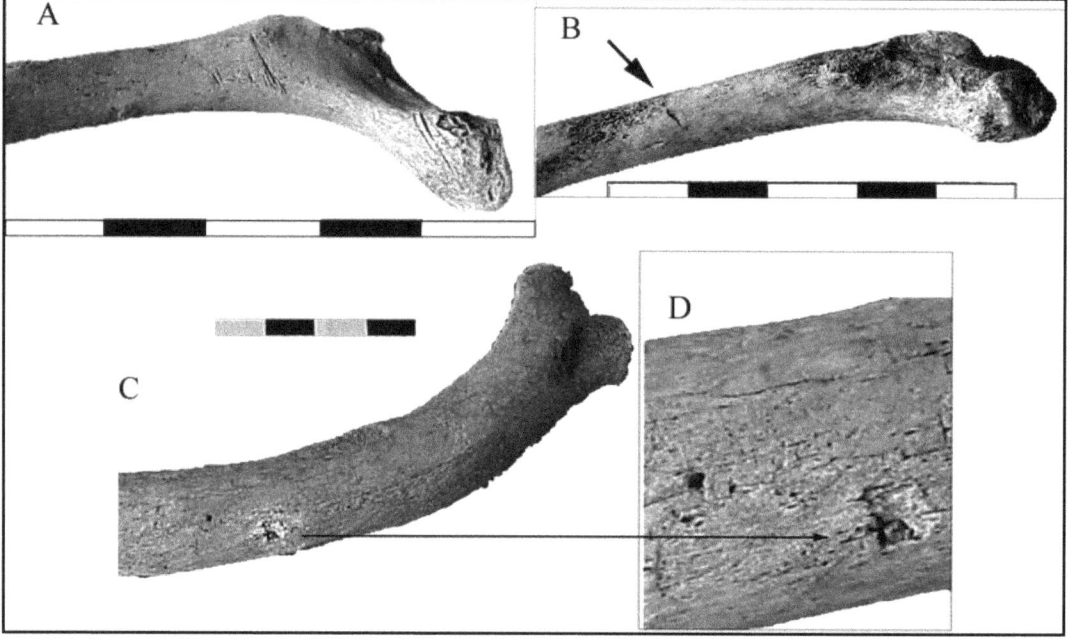

Figure 11. Sea lion ribs showing A) cut marks; B) lateral chop mark; C,D) embedded stone tip.

harpoon. Unless hitting a sharp and mortal arrow shot, the wounded prey may escape into the sea with no moving restriction such as a harpoon handle and sunk with the lungs fill up of water out of the hunter access. This turns in the lost of the prey and effort invested in the arrow. Nevertheless, if this sort of hunting was done frequently enough to leave archaeological evidence, the expectable success could not be irrelevant. Such probability of success leads to consider that the skill on the using of bows and its efficiency by the *Yamana* had to be higher than the one upcoming from the ethnographic sources.

In many cases the extraction techniques had been deduced extrapolating and inferring from the sex and age composition of the faunal remains and its representation of skeletal portions and topographic location of the sites (cf. Lyman, 1994). In the discussed case, sex and age composition, skeletal representation, extrapolation from the hunting instruments and topographic location jointly with all the archaeological context lead us to consider a hunting system based on the use of canoes and harpoons and now this picture is complemented with a non negligible opportunistic sea lion predation.

CONCLUSIONS

The possibility of documenting deep impacts would enable to verify, in other cases, techniques and strategies used for catching animal resources and sometimes the raw materials or instruments used for each activity. It has to be kept in mind that not all the macroscopically identifiable anthropic traces refer necessarily butchering or processing the prey. If we pretend to make more reliable archaeozoological analysis, we most emphasize the macro and microanalysis of the bone surfaces. In that way it would be possible to identify small remains of the instrument that originated the modifications observed and so certainly associate activities with instruments. Moreover, only the macroscopic analysis will enable to know the existing variability in the type of traces present in the archaeological record as well as its recurrence, intensity, orientation and location.

Analysis of marks on bones demonstrates that some unexpected and not specialized hunting techniques were usually employed on occasional close encounters between people and pinnipedia. Switching from very specialized hunting and maritime oriented to opportunistic behavior was normal. Contrasting ethnography and archaeology driven to a high analysis level has demonstrated that ethnographic information is biased: social and historically. It must therefore be contrasted more than though before. Direct induction from ethnography or from logical assumptions -even in very clear and apparently obvious cases of well-documented weapons as impressive as our harpoons- do not always conform with reality and that archaeozoological studies must be done to the highest detail (including detailed macroscopic analysis) before inducing general hunting techniques.

Authors' addresses

Jordi ESTÉVEZ
Departament d'Antropologia Social i Prehistòria
Universitat Autònoma de Barcelona
08193 Bellaterra, SPAIN

Laura MAMELI
Departament d'Antropologia Social i Prehistòria
Universitat Autònoma de Barcelona
08193 Bellaterra, SPAIN

Ernesto Luis PIANA
Programa de Antropología
CADIC
Ushuaia
Tierra del Fuego, ARGENTINA

Bibliography

BINFORD, L. R., 1981, *Bones: Ancient Men and modern myths*. New York: Academic Press.

BOUCHUD, J., 1974, Les traces de l' activité humaine sur les os fossiles. In *Colloques Méthodologie. appliquée à l'industrie de l' os préhistorique*. Sénanque, p. 27-33.

BROMAGE, T.G. & BOYDE, A., 1984, Microscopic Criteria for the Determination Directionality of Cutmarks on Bone. *American Journal of Physical Anthropology* 65, p. 359.

CLEMENTE, I., 1997, Los instrumentos liticos de Túnel VII: una aproximación etnoarqueológica. Bellaterra: Treballs d'Etnoarqueologia, 2 UAB-C.S.I.C.

ESTÉVEZ, J. & MARTÍNEZ, J., 1998, Archaeozoological researches at the Beagle Channel, Argentina. *Anthropozoologica*, 25-26 , p.237-246.

ESTEVEZ, J. & VILA, A. (eds.), 1995, *Encuentros en los conchales fueguinos*. Bellaterra: Treballs d'Etnoarqueologia, vol. 1. CSIC-UAB

ESTEVEZ, J. & VILA, A., 2000, Tierra del Fuego un lugar de encuentros. *Revista de Arqueología Americana*, 15 p. 187-219.

ESTEVEZ, J., 1995, Una historia interminada: l'estudi de restes animals arqueologiques davant un gran repte. *Cota 0*, 11, p. 13-24

ESTEVEZ, J., N. JUANS-MUNS, J. MARTINEZ, R. PIQUE & SCHIAVINI, A., 1995, Zooarqueología y Antracología: Estrategias de aprovechamiento de los recursos animales y vegetales en Túnel VII. In *Encuentros en los conchales fueguinos*. Coordinated by J. Estévez & A. Vila. Bellaterra: Treballs de Etnoarqueologia 1. CSIC-UAB, p. 143-163.

ESTEVEZ, J.; PIANA, E; SCHIAVINI,A.; JUAN-MUNS,N., 2001, Archaeological Analysis Of Shellmidden In The Beagle Channel,Tierra Del Fuego Island. *International Journal of Osteoarchaeology*. 11 p. 24-35.

HARTZ, N. & WINGE, H., 1906, Om uroxen fra Vig. Såret og draebt med flintvåben., *Aarbøger for Nordisk Oldkyndighed og Historie*. p. 225-236.

JUAN-MUNS, N., 1992, La pesca com alternativa economica per als Yamana, nómades canoers del canal Beagle. Bellaterra: Tesis doctoral inédita.Universidad Autónoma de Barcelona.

JUAN-MUNS, N., 1994, Fishing strategies in the Beagle Channel, Tierra del Fuego/Argentina: an ethnoarchaeological approach. *Archaeo-Ictiological Studies OFFA*, 51, p.313-316.

LYMAN, R.L., 1994, *Vertebrate Taphonomy*. Cambridge: Cambridge University Press.

MAMELI, L., 2000, *Análisis arqueoavifaunístico del yacimiento arqueológico Túnel VII (Tierra del Fuego, Argentina)*. Bellaterra: tesi de Llicenciatura. Universitat Autònoma de Barcelona.

MARTIN, H., 1907, *Recherches sur l'evolution du Mousterien dans le gisment de La Quina (Charente)*. París: Schleider Freres.

NOE-NYGAARD, I., 1974, Mesolithic hunting in Denmark illustraed by bone injuries caused by human weapons, *Journal of Archaeological Science*, 1, p. 217-218.

ORQUERA, L.A., & E.L. PIANA. (1995) "Túnel VII: la excavación" En: Encuentros en los conchales fueguinos.

Estévez, J. and A. Vila (Eds.) Treballs d'Etnoarqueologia, (1): 47-82. CSIC-UAB, Barcelona.

ORQUERA, L.A., & PIANA. E.L., 1999a, *La Arqueologia de la region del canal Beagle (Tierra del Fuego, República Argentina)*. Buenos Aires: Sociedad Argentina de Antropologia

ORQUERA, L.A., & PIANA. E.L., 1999b *La vida material y social de los Yamana*. Buenos Aires:Eudeba.

PIANA, E. L. & ESTEVEZ, J., 1995, Confección y significación de las industrias ósea y malacológica en Túnel VII", In *Encuentros en los conchales fueguinos*. Coordinated by J. Estévez & A. Vila. Bellaterra:Treballs de Etnoarqueologia 1. CSIC-UAB, p. 239-260.

PIANA, E. L. & ORQUERA, L. A., 1995, Túnel VII: la cronología. In *Encuentros en los conchales fueguinos*. COORDINATED BY J. ESTEVEZ & A. VILA. BELLATERRA:TREBALLS DE ETNOARQUEOLOGIA 1. CSIC-UAB, P.105-112..

PIANA, E. L., ESTEVEZ, J. & VILA, A., 2000, Lanashuaia: un sitio de canoeros del siglo pasado en la costa norte del canal Beagle. In *Desde el País de los Gigantes.Perspectivas arqueológicas en Patagonia* Río Gallegos: Universidad Nacional de la Patagonia. P. 455-469

PIANA, E.L., VÁZQUEZ, M. ÁLVAREZ, M. & RÚA, N., 2002 (In press), El Sitio Ajej I: Excavación de Rescate en la costa del canal Beagle In *Actas del XIV Congreso Nacional de Arqueologia Argentina. Rosario september, 2001*. Rosario: U.N.de Rosario.

PIANA, E.L., VILA, A., ORQUERA, L. A. & ESTEVEZ, J., 1992. Chronicles of Ona-ashaga: archaeology in the Beagle Channel (Tierra del Fuego, Argentina). *Antiquity*, vol. 66, n° 252 p.771-783.

POTTS, R. & SHIPMAN, P., 1981 Cutmarks made by stone tools on bones from Olduvai Gorge, Tanzania. *Nature* 291, p. 577-580.

SCHIAVINI, A.C.M., 1993, Los pinnípedos como recurso de los cazadores-recolectores marinos: el caso de Tierra del Fuego. *Latin American Antiquity* 4 (4), p.346-366.

SEMENOV, S.A., 1981, *Tecnología prehistórica*. Madrid: editorial Akal.

SHIPMAN, P. & ROSE, J.,1983, Evidence of Butchery an Hominid Activities at Torralba and Ambrona; An Evaluation Using Microscopic Techniques. *Journal of Archaeological Science* 10, p.465-474

TERRADES, X., E.A., 1999 Ethno-neglet or the contradiction between ethnohistorical sources and the archaeological record. The case of stone tools from the Yamana (Tierra del Fuego). IN Conard, N.J. (ed.) Tübingen: Urgeschichtliche Materialhefte

VILA, A. & ESTÉVEZ, J., 2000, Etnoarqueología como experimentación, In Mameli,L. & Pijoan,J. (eds.) *Reunión de Experimentación en Arqueologia*. Bellaterra: Treballs d'Arqueologia n° especial Universitat Autònoma de Barcelona 1999 Edición en CD ISSN: 1134-9263

VILA, A. & ESTEVEZ, J., 2001, Calibrando el método: arqueología en Tierra del Fuego. *Astigi Vetus,* 1, p.63-72

VILA, A., TERRADAS, X. CLEMENTE, I. & MANSUR, E. 1995 "La larga marcha: de roca a instrumento" In *Encuentros en los conchales fueguinos*. Coordinated by J. Estévez & A. Vila. Bellaterra:Treballs de Etnoarqueologia 1. CSIC-UAB, p. 261-274.

WALKER, P. L. & LONG, J. C., 1977, An experimental study of the morphological characteristics of tools marks. *American Antiquity,* 42, (4). p. 605-616.

OBSIDIENNE VERTE DE FEU-PATAGONIE, ¿SON UTILISATION CONSTANTE PENDANT 6000 ANS?

Alfredo PRIETO, Manuel SAN ROMAN, Flavia MORELLO & Charles STERN

Résumé. La découverte et l'exploitation de l'obsidienne verte en Feu-Patagonie sont étendues depuis l'apparition dans cette région des pêcheurs nomades, il y a 6000 ans, jusqu'aux temps historiques. L'origine de l'obsidienne est encore inconnue, même si les évidences géologiques et archéologiques la situent aux alentours du Fjord Otway, dans la région de Magellan au Chili.

Cette matière première accompagna les divers processus d'évolution et de changement de la technologie des pêcheurs nomades et de leurs voisins chasseurs terrestres. Malgré tout, son utilisation et échange ont perduré de façon invariable. On note une meilleure continuité d'utilisation au sein des groupes de pêcheurs nomades que dans ceux des peuples voisins du continent et des îles de la Terre de Feu. Alors que la principale source d'information reste le registre archéologique, il y a de très intéressants antécédents historiques et ethnographiques au sujet de son utilisation.

L'échange de l'obsidienne ne sera pas affecté jusqu'à l'arrivée des matières premières étrangères, comme le verre, et les métaux européens. On vous propose d'examiner son approvisionnement, utilisation, fonction, et sens entre les différents peuples de la région, sur une période de 6000 ans.

Abstract. The discovery and exploitation of green obsidian in Fuego Patagonia extended from the occurrence of canoe people in the region to historical times. The obsidian comes from an unknown source until now, but the archaeological evidence situates it in the surroundings of the Otway sound, Magallanes, Chile.

This raw material went along the various evolutive processes and changes in the technology of the canoe people and their neighbours terrestrials hunter-gatherers. Nevertheless there was more continuity in its use among canoe people than among their neighbours in the mainland and the Tierra del Fuego Island.

The main source of information is the archaeological record but there are interesting historical documents and ethnographic material about its use. The exchange of obsidian was not affected but until the arrival of Europeans items like glass and metals. Its acquisition use and function among the different groups in the region is assessed through a sequence of 6000 years.

ANTECEDENTS

L'intérêt autour de l'origine de l'obsidienne verte s'initie avec les fouilles de la Mission française, sous la direction de Joseph Emperaire, réalisées sur l'île Englefield dans le courant de l'année 1952 (Emperaire *et al.*, 1961). Dans cette île, le site du même nom, fait état d'une impressionnante quantité d'objets en obsidienne verte ce qui motiva Emperaire à s'intéresser aux origines de ce verre volcanique. Il remarque que la source, pourrait se trouver sur un passage d'indigènes qui aurait relié le fond du fjord avec le Détroit de Magellan.

L'élément que découvra Emperaire sur l'île Englefield, résulte faire partie d'une tradition plus large, d'anciens pêcheurs nomades que l'on situe aussi bien dans le détroit de Magellan que dans le canal Beagle. Ces sites, au moment ou apparurent les premiers indices de peuplement de pêcheurs nomades dans les archipels de Patagonie, présentent comme traits communs l'apparition d'arpons fabriqués sur os à base cruciforme, la consommation prédominante de mammifères marins, et, en ce qui concerne la péninsule de Brunswick-mer d'Otway, une industrie de pierres tallées à base d'obsidienne verte. Les sites de ce moment se situent entre 5.500 et 6.500 ans AP (avant le présent).

Des tentatives de situer l'origine de l'obsidienne verte n'obtiendront aucun résultat positif. Ont en était même arrivé à penser que la source avait pu s'épuiser. Cependant, avec la découverte du site "Punta Baja" par Dominique Legoupil, daté du XVIIème siècle de notre ère, il a été démontré que la source était encore en activité il y a 280 ans grâce à la présence sur le site d'une abondante production à base d'obsidienne, a coté de restes métalliques, dont certains métaux avaient d'ailleurs été transformés en outillage.

Au sein des pêcheurs nomades tardifs ont observe un changement dans la forme des pointes d'arpon, même si le mode de subsistance reste basé sur la chasse de mammifères et des ressources marines. Les arpons à base cruciforme ne s'utiliseront plus au profit de ceux à pointe simple ou double.

Dans le domaine des chasseurs terrestres des steppes patagoniques et fuégiennes, l'obsidienne verte avait déjà été identifiée par l'archéologue nord-américain Junius Bird lors des excavations des grottes Fell et Pali Aike, mais dans de tels faibles proportions qu'il n'y porta que très peu d'intérêt. L'intéressant de la découverte c'est, premièrement, sa situation dans la période Bird III (6500-4500 ans AP) et, deuxièmement, parce qu'elle fixe les débuts des échanges d'obsidienne verte entre chasseurs terrestres et marins. Cette information se trouve notamment renforcée par les observations de la Mission française dans ses excavations de la grotte Fell.

La comparaison des pourcentages de présence d'obsidienne verte en contexte pêcheurs marins et

Table 1. Pourcentage d'obsidienne verte en rapport aux autres matières premières.

Site Archéologique	Obsidienne verte	Référence
Cueva Fell	0.02 %	Schidlowsky 1999; Stern 2000[1]
Pali Aike	1.2 %	Stern 2000[2]
Cañadón Leona	0.5 %	Stern 2000
Englefield	96 %	Schidlowsky 1999
Bahía Colorada	88 %	Schidlowsky 1999
Bahía Buena	97 %	Schidlowsky 1999
Punta Santa Ana	43 %	Schidlowsky 1999
Punta Baja	>90% (n=2537,~4,8Kg)	Legoupil 1989

Table 2: Démonstration comparative entre le poids total de matériaux à base d'obsidienne verte et la superficie fouillée dans différents sites de la Patagonie méridionale.

SITE	POIDS obsidienne verte (g.)	SUPERFICIE (m^2)	GRS. x M^2
Punta Baja	4805	90	53.4
Río Verde 1 (fouille)	99.1	2	49.6
Angostura Titus	1.5	4	0.4
Puesto de la Sal	0.9	0.25	3.6
Camden 4	15	0.25	60
Camden 3	0.7	0.125	5.6
Bahía Laredo 1 A	47.5	8	5.9
Alero Peggy Bird	19.4	7	2.8
Río Hollemberg	27	50	0.54

chasseurs terrestres est donnée à titre indicatif, dans ces sites d'une ancienneté moyenne d'environ 6000 ans. Le but, est de délimiter la zone ou l'on pourrait déterminer l'origine de l'obsidienne verte et confirmer l'hypothèse que l'exploitation et les échanges de cette matière première lithique ont dû s'effectuer sur le territoire des populations de pêcheurs (cf. Table 1).

Dans la steppe, il existe plusieurs sites archéologiques datés où l'on a identifié l'obsidienne verte. Une sépulture avec cet élément dans la baie Laredo datée de 1570 ans AP, plusieurs éléments dans le site "Cañadón de la Leona" daté à 2280 AP (Prieto et al. 1998), et dans "Tom Gould", dans la partie datée entre 4.560 et 1.280 ans AP (Massone, 1981). Les autres sites datés dans le secteur des canaux sont "Angostura Titus", ou encore "SK14", dans la mer de Skyring et qui avoisinent les 1000 ans AP (Legoupil, 2000).

Sur la côte Est de la mer de Skyring a été détecté un petit gisement que l'on peut attribuer à un petit campement de chasseurs terrestres. Ce site, nommé "Rio verde 1" (n°18), daté vers 280 plus ou moins 60 ans de notre ère, se caractérise par une prédominance de restes de Guanaco (Lama guanicoe), la présence d'épiphyses d'os longs de Guanaco avec coupe périmetrique, caractéristique exclusive d'un contexte de chasseurs terrestres, et la présence d'un morceau de fer. L'aspect le plus notable du site est l'abondante présence de restes en obsidienne verte (cf. table 2). Cette découverte, nous permet de formuler des questions relatives à l'approvisionnement et échange d'obsidienne de la part des groupes tardifs ou historiques de chasseurs du continent et, en plus, d'avancer des hypothèses sur les éventuelles scènes de contacts et de relations inter-ethniques générées par ces échanges.

Il est également important de signaler, l'existence de sites en contexte pêcheurs nomades, comme "Ponsonby" ou "Km 44", daté à 4500 et 3000 ans respectivement, situés proche de l'ère de prédominance de l'obsidienne verte et

---

[1] Dans le 12% de restes d'obsidienne signalé par Stern (2000), il faut inclure à l'obsidienne verte la noire et la grise mouchetée. Selon l'analyse de Schidlowsky (1999), qui a révisé les collections d'Emperaire (1959), Bird (1969; 1970) et Fell (1958), le pourcentage d'obsidienne verte par rapport aux autres matières premières serait inférieur au 0,02% mentionné dans la table 1.

[2] Les pourcentages d'Stern (2000) ne séparent pas l'obsidienne verte des autres types fréquents en Patagonie, comme par exemple l'obsidienne noire et grise mouchetée.

qui ne contiennent pas ou ne présentent que de rares pièces de ce verre volcanique.

REGISTRES ETHNOGRAPHIQUES

L'utilisation de l'obsidienne en contexte pêcheurs nomades subsiste jusqu'aux temps historiques comme il a déjà été fait mention, information que l'on retrouve dans les collections ethnographiques. On sait d'une pointe de projectile du Musée Britannique, et d'une pointe de flèche de ce matériau donnée au Musée Régional de Magellan et provenant probablement des Selk'nam, c'est à dire de la Terre de Feu. En plus, on possède un récit de Giglioli de 1867 (Corvette italienne Magenta), qui décrit l'utilisation d'objets à base d'obsidienne verte entre les pêcheurs nomades dans la zone du l'Ille Carlos III: *«on signale la présence d'une pointe de flèche d'obsidienne verte obtenue des fuégiens du canal messier»* (Giglioli 1875:950). Cette référence rend compte de la présence la plus nord-occidentale de cette matière première.

Dans un autre sens, la distribution spatiale des découvertes d'obsidienne verte est un point important à considérer, générant une zone d'échange avec de grandes distances comme celle du Canal Messier (à 500km de la mer d'Otway), et "Túnel 1" au Canal Beagle (à 350km) dans l'axe Nord-Sud. Dans le même temps, il existe des témoignages de la présence d'obsidienne jusque dans l'entrée Atlantique du Détroit de Magellan.

PROSPECTIONS GEO-ARCHÉLOGIQUES

Les découvertes les plus intéressantes se sont développées sur la côte de l'île Riesco. A ce propos, il a été décrit un ensemble très intéressant de gisements imputables à des occupations tardives de pêcheurs, situées 1 à 2 mètres au-dessus du niveau de la mer dans la première terrasse marine, qui incluent de grandes pièces en obsidienne. Dans un de ces gisements situés sur la côte du canal Fitz-Roy, s'est récupéré un bâton d'obsidienne qui est devenu la pièce décrite la plus grande jusqu'à ce jour.

Dans l'intention de mieux connaître le contexte géologique de la formation d'obsidienne, et d'aider à préciser le lieu de la source des datations K-Ar (Potassium-Argon) ont été réalisées sur l'obsidienne et les formations innées des alentours de la mer d'Otway.

La datation de l'obsidienne verte a donné un résultat compris entre 16,8 millions d'années plus ou moins 0,6 millions, et 17,1 plus ou moins 0,6 millions d'années. Une datation K-Ar, pour l'intrusive du Mont Caleta, révéla un âge de 19,7 plus ou moins 0,6 millions d'années, alors que la datation d'un échantillon de digue, de "Punta Baja" a déterminé, 18,3 plus ou moins 0,6 millions d'années. Ceci implique, que les corps innés signalés précédemment se sont formés également dans le même événement magmatique, le Burdigalien du Miocène récent, de la même manière que l'obsidienne verte. C'est tout à fait probable que la source de l'obsidienne se trouve dans un axe Nord-Sud défini para ces *locus* de corps innés, et les cordillères Pinto, Paine, Baguales, et Fitz-Roy vers le nord.

DISCUSSION

La taille bifaciale et les stéréotypes de fabrication sont importants sur les sites de la culture Englefield, au même titre que l'exploitation intensive de l'obsidienne. Cela se reflète également dans les sites plus tardifs comme "Punta Baja", bien que les formes et les objets souhaités varient, produit de l'effet de la taille (Schidlowsky, 1999). Cela nous indique qu'on peut définir des traditions culturelles autour de l'exploitation et de l'utilisation de l'obsidienne verte. Pour autant, il est important de connaître ces traditions de la même manière que de pouvoir reconnaître les contextes culturels au sein desquels l'obsidienne est minoritairement représentée ou encore absente.

Partant de la supposition que les chasseurs terrestres ont eu un accès très restreint, voire nul, à la source, c'est à dire limité aux échanges avec les groupes de pêcheurs nomades, il est probable qu'à chaque fois dans les contextes continentaux de Patagonie et Terre de Feu cette matière première a été rare et rentabilisée au maximum, comme un produit de qualité et valorisé (*cf.* tables 1 et 2). Au contraire, dans un contexte de pêcheurs nomades, spécialement dans les zones proches de la frange de localisation de la source on devrait s'attendre à une plus grande abondance du matériau. Maintenant, il convient de se demander pourquoi il y a une quasi-absence totale d'obsidienne à "Ponsomby", "Km44", "Camden 2", et quelques sites des mers d'Otway et Skyring.

Alors, il apparaît intéressant de débattre, même si cela doit être bref, de la virtuelle absence d'obsidienne verte dans les registres du gisement archéologique de Ponsomby (80 km pour voie maritime du Englefield). La couche B de "Ponsonby", en ce qui concerne les matériaux lithiques, est identique au composant ancien de "Lancha Packewaia" dans le canal Beagle, en ce qui concerne en particulier les grandes pointes de projectiles bifaciales, allongées, foliacées, et dentelées (Orquera *et al.*, 1977; Piana, 1984). D'un autre coté, c'est le second composant de "Túnel 1", daté à 6200 ans, associé à la découverte d'une pointe, et 5 éclats en obsidienne verte, qui représentent un site proche culturellement, des sites de l'île Englefield. La similitude entre "Ponsomby" et "Lancha Packewaia" apparaît surprenant, quand on sait que Ponsonby se trouve plus proche de Englefield que du Beagle, ce qui contraste avec la présence d'obsidienne verte dans le second composant de "Túnel 1". On pourrait penser qu'il s'agit d'un autre groupe, avec une tradition culturelle dans laquelle n'était pas connue la source de l'obsidienne verte, et où il n'y avait pas d'intérêt pour obtenir la roche directement ou par échange. Un chantier similaire à celui de "Ponsomby" se trouve dans le gisement "km44", où il n'y a pas non plus d'obsidienne, et qui est daté de 2960 ans AP. La même situation se présente sur le site "Camden 2", avec une ancienneté de 3030 ans AP, et sans obsidienne[3]. Pour sa

---

[3] Camden 2 est situé sur une terrasse marine de 4 a 5 snm, juste en haut du site Candem 3, décrit par Lucille Johnson (1976). Ce gisement est

part, le site le plus ancien de la mer de Skyring (N° 29: 5.312 ans AP) ne contient pas non plus d'obsidienne, même s'il est connu bien peu de ce chantier où l'excavation a été très réduite (0.5m^2), (Legoupil, 2000). D'autres pointes sciées, bien que sans contextes spécifiques, ont été rencontrées sur l'île Dawson, le Rio Hollemberg, et l'île de los Muertos, les deux derniers dans la province de Última Esperanza.

En définitive, à partir des informations archéologiques présentées jusqu'à présent on semble démontrer que la source d'obsidienne a été à disposition des pêcheurs nomades depuis la consolidation de ce mode vie et jusqu'au septième millénaire. Mais son exploitation semble être interrompue entre quatre et deux miles ans avant le présent. Comme nous le signalions, l'hypothèse est que cette tradition aurait pu se suspendre ou être contemporaine à l'arrivée de nouveaux groupes dans la zone, altérant alors le rythme d'échange vers la Pampa, o par quelconque variation de l'habitat (vulcanisme récent), comme l'indique dans une certaine mesure Stern (2000).

Dans ce sens, on observe dans le contexte archéologique de chasseurs terrestres un laps de temps, vu que l'obsidienne verte n'apparaît pas dans les matériaux de la période Fell IV de la séquence continentale de Bird (sites Fell, Pali Aike et Cañadón Leona; 4500-1500 ans AP). Le seul site daté correspondant à cet espace de temps et présentant de l'obsidienne verte, c'est celui de la "Laguna Thomas Gould". En général, cette matière lithique réapparaît dans la sous-période suivante (Fell V), dans laquelle on la trouve dans les sites des canaux comme dans certains gisements tardifs de Skyring, ou dans l'Angostura Titus. Cette conclusion se fonde sur la base de certaines datations et de sa position en terrasses côtières, qui n'étaient pas disponibles auparavant, en raison de la montée du niveau de la mer à l'Holocène, vers les 5000 ans AP.

Cette dernière information est un aspect important à signaler, car se complémente à de possibles changements de végétation, comme les avancées et retraits des forêts, il se peut que se soit la montée du niveau de la mer dans les débuts de l'Holocène tardif qui ait occulté, et par la suite révélée de nouveau, la source de l'obsidienne verte. Cet aspect, se contredit malgré tout, avec la supposition que la source se trouvait près de la côte, dans un lieu qui aurait pu être découvert facilement par les groupes anciens de pêcheurs nomades, à une hauteur supérieure a 15 mètres au-dessus du niveau de la mer, dû aux conditions paléo-environnementales de la période considérée. De toutes façons, ces spéculations sont complexes, en raison des changements spécifiques qui peuvent arriver à une moindre échelle dans la région et même dans le paysage au niveau local.

Plus en avant dans le temps, c'est à dire entre les 1500 ans AP et les temps historiques, on enregistre de nouveau une

entièrement recouvert d'herbes et d'arbres son espace est délimité par des longs piquets ou s'est déroulée une fouille de 50 x 50 cm durant laquelle ont a récolté une grande quantité de restes osseux de loups de mer et quelques matériaux lithiques.

tradition culturelle associée à l'exploitation de l'obsidienne verte au sein des groupes pêcheurs nomades, de "Punta Baja", et son échange avec des groupes de chasseurs terrestres sur "Rio verde 1". Cette tradition a dû subsister jusqu'à la première moitié du 20ème siècle, comme le démontre le site sous-actuel de "Caleta 2", datée à 110 ans avant le présent, et les informations ethno-historiques qui signalent sa brutale disparition vers le milieu du XIXème siècle et les débuts du XXème. Il est intéressant de voir comment, peu à peu, le verre et les métaux commencèrent à gagner du terrain sur l'obsidienne, que ce soit chez les chasseurs terrestres (Aoniken et Selk'nam), ou chez les pêcheurs nomades eux-mêmes. La présence d'une lame de cuivre empoignée trouvée sur "Punta Baja" signifie que son propriétaire a pu pour le moins remplacer l'obsidienne ou les couteaux-coquillage comme outil tranchant par un couteau de cuivre, qui pouvait en plus effiler continuellement avant de l'épuiser. Après révision de la littérature ethnohistorique, on déduit que les pêcheurs nomades étaient avides de matériaux comme le verre et le métal, qu'ils changeaient pour des peaux et d'autres produits du détroit de Magellan. Cela marquerait la fin de l'exploitation utile de la source et l'oublie de cette tradition.

Un autre aspect à considérer c'est que l'exploitation de l'obsidienne verte a dû se restreindre au moment de l'année où les indigènes se déplaçaient dans les eaux intérieures de la mer d'Otway, possiblement en été et automne, Ceci, en tenant compte que la source devrait se situer dans un endroit de la frange centrale des mers d'Otway et Skyring, et qu'il ait été démontré une possible saisonnalité dans l'utilisation de sites tardifs de cette zone, comme "Punta Baja"(Legoupil, 1989).

A ce sujet, Annette Laming-Emperaire signale (Laming-Emperaire, 1972), en se basant sur les prospections archéologiques sur la région, qu'on peut apprécier l'existence de deux franges d'occupations intensives et une zone intermédiaire vide. Les franges les plus utilisées seraient celles des côtes les plus occidentales des archipels, et celles des côtes continentales. L'occupation de "Punta Baja" entre les mois de janvier et juillet nous permet de déduire que le reste de l'année les indigènes ont pu sortir vers le détroit, et de là vers les *roquerios* de la côte occidentale, où ils avaient l'habitude de chasser abondamment les loups de mer. La présence et la quantité d'obsidienne verte sur la côte pacifique pourraient corroborer en partie ces affirmations, du fait de la mobilité des pêcheurs marins, et de son propre moyen de navigation -le canot-, qui leur permettait de disposer d'un mode de transport pour des poids importants, par exemple, depuis une réserve d'obsidienne s'ils estimaient qu'elle avait de la valeur. Cependant, elles sont très rares les recherches développées actuellement dans les archipels occidentaux de cette zone, bien qu'avant de se lancer sur une étude de ce caractère il serait intéressant de poser le problème de l'utilisation et de la fonctionnalité des objets en obsidienne verte dans les contextes de pêcheurs marins tardifs. Dans ce sens, la taille bifaciale paraît être prédominante, ce qui permet d'évaluer la fonction des pointes, spécialement à "Punta Baja", en pensant qu'elles étaient destinées à la chasse de mammifères terrestres comme le Guanaco et le Huemul (*Hippocamelus bisulcus*). En poursuivant avec cette idée, il faudrait se demander quel était l'objectif d'emporter des pointes de projectiles d'obsidienne ou cette matière première dans des déplacements nomades et saisonniers vers le versant occidental des canaux de la Patagonie et de la Terre de Feu.

Traduction: Laurent Salles. Punta Arenas, septembre 2001.

Adresses des auteurs

Alfredo PRIETO, Manuel SAN ROMAN,
Flavia MORELLO
Instituto de la Patagonia,
Universidad de Magallanes
Punta Arenas, CHILE

Charles STERN
University of Colorado
Boulder, CO USA

Bibliographie

BIRD, J., 1980. Investigaciones Arqueológicas en la Isla Isabel, Estrecho de Magallanes. *Anales del Instituto de la Patagonia*, 11:75-87.

BIRD, J., 1993. *Viajes y Arqueología en Chile Austral*. Ediciones de la Universidad de Magallanes.

BORRERO, L. & FRANCO N., 2001. Las Colecciones Líticas del Museo Británico. *Anales del Instituto de la Patagonia*, serie cs. Hs. N° 29. En prensa.

EMPERAIRE, J. & LAMING A., 1961. Les Gisements des Iles Englefield et Vivian dans la Mer d'Otway (Patagonie Australe). *Journal de la Société de Américanistes* n.s. 50:7-75.

EMPERAIRE, J.; A. LAMING & REICHLEN H., 1963. La Grotte Fell et autres sites de la région volcanique de la Patagonie Chilienne. *Journal de la Société des Américanistes* 52:167-229.

GIGLIOLI, E., 1875. *Viaggio ntorno al globo della pirocorvetta italiana Magenta*. Maisner e Cia. Editori. Milano.

GUSINDE, M., 1990. *Los Indios de Tierra del Fuego, Los Halakwulup*. Tomo III, vol. I. Centro Argentino de Etnología Americana.

JOHNSON, L., 1978. Informe sobre una Prospección Arqueológica en Magallanes. *Anales del Instituto de la Patagonia*, 7: 87-94.

LAMING-EMPERAIRE, A., 1965. Mission Archeologique Francaise au Chili Austral. *Journal de la Société des Americanistes* 54: 127-135.

LAMING-EMPERAIRE, A., 1967. Cadre Chronologique Provisoire de la Préhistoire de Patagonie et de Terre de Feu Chiliennes. *Boletín del Museo Nacional de Historia* Natural, XXX: 221-236.

LAMING-EMPERAIRE, A., 1972. Los Sitios Arqueológicos de los Archipiélagos de la Patagonia Occidental. *Anales del Instituto de la Patagonia* III(1-2):87-96.

LEGOUPIL, D., 1980. Reconocimiento Arqueológico de la Costa Sur del Seno Otway. *Anales del Instituto de la Patagonia* 11:91-99.

LEGOUPIL, D., 1980-81. Mission Préhistorique de Patagonie. Août 1980 - Janvier 1981 RAPPORT. Ministère des Affaires Etrangères & CNRS. MS.

LEGOUPIL, D., 1988. Ultimas Consideraciones sobre las Dataciones del Sitio de Isla Englefield (Seno de Otway). *Anales del Instituto de la Patagonia*, Serie Cs. Humanas 18:95-98.

LEGOUPIL, D., 1989. *Ethno-Archéologie dans les Archipels de Patagonie: les Nomades Marins de Punta Baja*. Editions Recherche sur les Civilisations. "Mémoire" n° 84.

LEGOUPIL, D., 1993-94. El Archipiélago del Cabo de Hornos y la Costa Sur de la Isla Navarino: Poblamiento y Modelo Económicos. *Anales del Instituto de la Patagonia*, Serie Cs. Humanas 22:101-122.

LEGOUPIL, D., 1997. *Bahía Colorada (Ile Englefield)*. Recherche sur les Civilisations, Paris.

LEGOUPIL, D. & FONTUGNE M., 1997. El Poblamiento Marítimo en los Archipiélagos de Patagonia: Núcleos Antiguos y Dispersión Reciente. *Anales del Instituto de la Patagonia*, Serie Cs. Humanas 25: 75-87.

MAPA GEOLÓGICO DE MAGALLANES, 1978. SERNAGEOMIN.

MASSONE, M., 1981a. Arqueología de la Región de Pali-Aike (Patagonia Meridional Chilena). *Anales del Instituto de la Patagonia* 12:95-124.

MASSONE, M., 1989-90. Investigaciones Arqueológicas en Laguna Thomas Gould. *Anales del Instituto de la Patagonia*, Serie Cs. Humanas 19:87-100.

MORELLO, F., 1999. *Cazadores Terrestres del Holoceno Medio y Temprano en Tierra del Fuego: Marazzi 1, una Discusión Abierta*. Memoria de Título, Universidad de Chile, Facultad de Ciencias Sociales, Depto Antropología. MS.

ORQUERA, L. A.; A. SALAS; E. PIANA & HAYDEE A., 1977. *Lancha Packewaia. Arqueología de los Canales Fueguinos*. Editorial Huemul, Buenos Aires.

ORQUERA, L & PIANA E., Composición tipologica y datos tecnomorfologicos de la región del canal Beagle. *Relaciones de la Sociedad Argentina de Antropología* XVII/1: 59-82.

ORTIZ-TRONCOSO, 1975. Los Yacimientos de Punta Santa Ana y Bahía Buena (Patagonia Austral). Excavaciones y Fechados Radiocarbónicos. *Anales del Instituto de la Patagonia* VI(1-2):93-122.

ORTIZ-TRONCOSO, 1979. Punta Santa Ana et Bahía Buena: deux Gisements sur une ancienne ligne de rivage dans le détroit de Magellan. *Journal de la Société des Américanistes* 60(6):133-204.

ORTIZ-TRONCOSO, 1980. Dos Fechados Radiocarbónicos para el Fiordo Silva Palma, Península de Brunswick, Patagonia Austral. *Anales del Instituto de la Patagonia* 11:89-90.

PIANA, E., 1984. *Arrinconamiento o Adaptación en Tierra del Fuego*. En: Ensayos de Antropología Argentina, Editorial del Belgrano.

PIGEOT, N., 1989. Les Techniques de Taille. En: Legoupil, D. *Ethno-Archéologie dans les Archipels de Patagonie: les nomades marins de Punta Baja*. Ediciones de Recherche sur les Civilisations, "Mémoire" n° 84.

PRIETO, A., 1988 Cazadores-Recolectores del Istmo de Brunswick. *Anales del Instituto de la Patagonia*, Serie Cs. Humanas 18:113-132.

PRIETO, A.; F. MORELLO; R. CARDENAS & CHRISTENSEN M., 1998. Cañadón Leona: A Sesenta Años de su Descubrimiento. *Anales del Instituto de la Patagonia*, Serie Cs. Humanas 26:83-106.

SCHIDLOWSKY, V., 1999. *Comportements Techno-Economiques et Identité Culturelle des Premiers Chasseurs Maritimes et des Chasseurs Terrestres de Patagonie Australe. Contribution de la Technologie Lithique*. Thèse du Doctorat, Université Paris I, en Préhistoire, Ethnologie et Anthropologie. 3 volúmenes. MS.

STERN, C. & PRIETO A., 1991. Obsidiana Verde de los Sitios Arqueológicos en los Alrededores del Seno Otway, Magallanes, Chile. *Anales del Instituto de la Patagonia*, Serie Cs. Humanas 20:139-144.

STERN, C., 2000. Fuentes de los Artefactos de Obsidiana en los Sitios Arqueológicos de las Cuevas de Pali Aike y Fell, y Cañadón La Leona, en Patagonia Austral. *Anales del Instituto de la Patagonia*, serie Cs. Hs., 28: 251-263 (2000).

UTILISATION OPPORTUNISTE D'OUTILS EN PIERRE CHEZ LES TURKANA (NORD KENYA)

Jean-Philip BRUGAL & Vincent MOURRE

Résumé: Les Turkana habitent actuellement l'Ouest du lac du même nom au Nord du Kenya, dans une région aride de la Rift Valley. Ces nilotiques possèdent une économie pastorale et des traditions guerrières ; chasse, pêche et un peu d'agriculture complètent cette économie. Lors de recherches sur les formations Plio-Pléistocènes dans cette région (WTAP), nous avons souvent observé des camps abandonnés et débuté un travail de relevé des structures (hutte, foyer, etc.) et vestiges (faune, etc.). Plusieurs types d'occupations, depuis des haltes courtes jusqu'à des campements plus importants ont ainsi été observés, localisés dans divers biotopes de plateaux et de vallées. Les déplacements sont fréquents, plus ou moins saisonniers, en fonction des ressources en eau et en pâturages. Lors de ces travaux, nous avons constaté l'utilisation de roches, débitées ou façonnées à partir des nombreux blocs d'origine volcanique présents dans toute la zone du Rift. La taille de ces blocs est généralement ponctuelle, destinée à l'obtention de supports coupants, pas ou très rarement retouchés, et d'utilisation d'outils lourds sur blocs. Ces outils correspondent à des utilisations opportunistes en vue d'activité de boucherie dans la plupart des cas, parfois de traitement de peau. Nous présenterons une brève description des habitats et de leurs organisations, ainsi qu'une analyse de ces outils de fortune.

Abstract: The Turkana are located in an arid zone at the West of Lake Turkana (ex. Lake Rudolf), in the Rift Valley, North Kenya. They are Nilotic people with pastoralist-base economy and warrior traditions, completed by hunting, fishing and limited agriculture. During fieldworks on the Plio-Pleistocene formation (West Turkana Archaeological Project - WTAP), we have regularly observed abandoned settlements and then started a systematic survey and record of different structures (huts, hearths, etc.) and remains (faunal, lithics, etc.). Several types of occupations are depicted, since short stations to more important camp, located in various biotopes. The degree of mobility is high, according to their need of water and pastures. Following this study, we have noticed the use of stones, knapped and shaped from the numerous volcanic rocks abundant in the Rift valley. The use of stones is generally punctual, and aims at obtaining sharp edges, rarely retouched, as well as heavy tools. These are opportunistic actions completed to accomplish butchering and hide-working activities. A few indications are given about habitats and settlement system with more details about the use of stone-tool materials.

Les Turkana forment une tribu localisée sur la rive Ouest du lac du même nom au Nord Kenya. Le lac Turkana (anciennement Lac Rudolf) s'étend sur près de 250 km dans la Vallée du Rift et jouxte au nord les frontières de l'Ethiopie et du Soudan. Cette région est bien connue pour ses formations plio-pléistocènes (Omo, Koobi Fora, Nachukui) ayant livré les plus anciennes traces d'activités humaines, de plus de 2 Millions d'années (i.e., Leakey, 1981 : Roche et al., 1999) ainsi que de nombreux restes humains (*Australopithecus*, *Homo*) et des associations animales fossiles. Dans le cadre d'un projet de recherche conjoint entre le National Museum de Nairobi (resp. M. Kibunja) et la Mission Préhistorique Française au Kenya (M.A.E., resp. H. Roche), des prospections suivies de fouilles extensives sont effectuées depuis quelques années dans l'Ouest Turkana (West Turkana Archaeological Project, WTAP). La formation de Nachukui, épaisse de près de 730m, livre d'importants gisements archéologiques (Oldowayen, Acheuléen) qui nous informent sur les comportements techniques et de subsistance des premiers hominidés (2,4-1,5 Ma).

Lors des missions de terrain du WTAP, nous avons eu l'occasion d'observer à maintes reprises des structures et habitats, abandonnés ou encore actifs, de Turkana. C'est ainsi qu'un certain nombre d'observations et de relevés de ces structures ou de ces campements a commencé, essentiellement sur les sites désertés, actuels ou sub-actuels (J.P.B.), notant à la fois les distributions spatiales intra- et inter-sites dans la région d'étude. C'est également au cours de ces prospections relevant d'une approche à la fois taphonomique et (ethno) archéozoologique que nous avons constaté l'existence d'objets travaillés en roche dure à la fois à l'intérieur des campements mais aussi de manière dispersée, en association ou non, avec des structures plus isolées dans l'environnement. Outre les études spatiales et faunistiques (Brugal, en prép.), nous voudrions présenter ici les résultats des relevés et analyses typo-technologiques assorties de remarques fonctionnelles sur cette panoplie d'artefacts lithiques utilisés de nos jours par les pasteurs-guerriers Turkana.

LES NOBLES SAUVAGES

C'est ainsi que M. Amin (1981) surnomme les Turkana, ou pasteurs-nomades de la Mer de Jade comme dans le superbe volume de N. Pavit (1997). C'est à ses ouvrages, ainsi qu'a ceux de A. Fedders et C. Salvadori (1989), J. Adamson (1967), D.K. Jones (1984) et R. Leakey et R. Lewin (1979) que nous emprunterons les données générales concernant cette ethnie, complétés par nos propres observations et enquêtes. Les Turkana sont des Nilotiques vivant essentiellement en plaines - comme les Maasai, Samburu et Merille - mais pouvant également se trouver sur les hauts plateaux - comme les Pokot -, vers l'Uganda. Ils se situent dans la zone ouest du lac alors que des ethnies couchitiques se trouvent à l'est du lac (Rendille, Gabbra, Boran, Somali).

La population Turkana regroupe entre 200 et 250 000 locuteurs qui couvrent un territoire d'env. 70 000 km².

Ils se partageraient suivant 19 territoires avec moins d'une trentaine de «clans». En réalité, leur système socio-économique n'est pas fondé sur un vrai clanisme et il n'existe pas d'organisation sociale élevée. Le système de classes d'âge est moins développé que dans d'autres ethnies (comme chez les hommes Maasai : ex. les Morans) ; il se limite à un système de moitiés organisés en fonction de générations (Pavit, 1997). L'unité de base est de type familial. Ils sont décrits comme «opportuniste, endurant, individualiste, peu structurés,...» et les enquêtes ethnographiques ne sont pas toujours aisées. Les principales ressources sont leur bétail et l'eau, et les objectifs vitaux répondent en terre (espace) et bétail.

Les Turkana sont des nomades vivant principalement d'élevage, en particulier de bovinés, mais aussi d'ovicaprinés (mouton, chèvre), des dromadaires et des ânes. Les deux premiers fournissent viande, graisse et peau. Par exemple, la queue des moutons contient beaucoup de gras qui est utilisé de diverses manières contre le soleil (peau, containers en bois). Les équidés sont utilisés pour le portage et il n'est pas rare de rencontrer de grands troupeaux rassemblés lors des saisons sèches dans la zone de terrain ; ils sont souvent mangés lors de crise. Les camélidés sont exploités pour le lait et servent dans les cérémonies et échanges entre familles ; ils peuvent être mangés lors d'occasions cérémonielles majeures. Les chiens sont rares et sont de petite taille. Les Turkana possèdent également des traditions guerrières et sont expansionnistes. Ils vivent ainsi de raids ainsi que de chasse, de collecte voire de pêche pour les groupes les plus sédentarisés autour du lac. La chasse a été intensive ces dernières dizaines d'années et les proies potentielles sont devenues rares et peu diversifiés. De nombreuses espèces sont collectées et chassées depuis les tortues, serpents, crocodiles jusqu'au porc-épic ou à la gazelle, et des carnivores. De plus, ils cultivent ponctuellement quelques pieds de millet et de maïs (juste avant la saison des pluies, dans des dépressions) ; l'agriculture reste toujours marginale. Les populations proches du lac sont plus sédentaires avec de plus nombreuses cultures (relation avec l'eau) et un régime plus aquatique (poissons), qui peut fournir une ressource plus stable en cas de disette.

De manière générale, le degré de mobilité est élevé en relation avec les besoins en eau et en pâturages se modifiant selon des rythmes saisonniers ou pluri-saisonniers, et souvent plusieurs fois dans l'année. Les besoins sont d'ailleurs différents entre des zones d'herbages (bovins, ovins), et des zones ou les feuillages (souvent d'épineux) sont plus denses (chèvre, dromadaire). Le climat est de type semi-aride et il n'est pas rare de voir plusieurs années sans eau entraînant de sérieuses famines et des déplacements importants de groupes humains. Cette mobilité dans la population, au sein des territoires et des familles, s'exprime par les 23 verbes existant sur la façon de marcher. Ces mouvements ont des répercussions dans la composition des groupes dont l'unité de base est de type familial. Une famille est composée d'un homme, d'une ou plus femmes, d'enfants et d'«anciens» (grand-parents, oncle, ...). Des regroupements de plusieurs familles (2 à 5 dans la région d'étude) constituent les campements les plus importants.

Il n'existe pas de poterie et, a priori pas d'artefacts lithiques. Toutefois des roches sont employées comme meule, et nous avons pu constater l'usage fréquent de pierre comme percuteur, notamment sur enclume (cas du concassage des noix des palmiers Doum : *Hyphaene compressa* (=*H.multiformis, H.thebaica*) (Noad et Birnie, 1989). Le métal est utilisé, bien que les Turkana ne soient pas des forgerons, et se procurent la matière première nécessaire auprès d'autres marchés[1]. Ce métal est employé comme couteau (couteau circulaire de poignet ou semi-circulaire) ou pour les lances (cf.*infra*) ; d'autres objets en métal sont également disponibles (machettes, hache). En dehors de l'aspect alimentaire, beaucoup de sous-produits animaux sont travaillés : cuir (ex. pour les boucliers), corne, sabots, os, ligaments, plumes (parure masculine). Parmi les végétaux, le bois est une denrée importante, non seulement pour le feu et les structures d'habitats ou de portage, mais également pour la confection des lances, javelines et bâtons, ou gourdes, bols...complétés par des graines et des noix. De nombreux ustensiles sont en bois, certains sont en métal et on rencontre relativement peu de plastiques.

Région d'Etude

La zone couverte par les recherches de la WTAP est localisée autour de 4°N et 35°E, le long du lac Turkana et couvre une surface d'environ 600 km². La majeure part des terrains d'études (où se placent les gisements plio-pléistocènes) se situe entre 8 et 15 km de la rive du lac. La zone péri-lacustre est ici bordée de nombreux palmiers Doum riches en noix et il n'est pas rare de rencontrer des enfants et des femmes en faisant la collecte, avec des zones d'activités spécifiques pour casser ces noix. Elles sont retrouvées dans les sites plus éloignés. Les piémonts sont parsemés de collines et petits plateaux (alt.env. 100 m) avec un réseau hydrologique dense (rivières sèches ou *lagas*). Ces rivières sont des voies de déplacement privilégiées bien que de nombreux passages existent entre les différentes 'vallées'. La faune locale est très appauvrie (surchasse ?) et nous avons seulement recensé des duiker, lièvre, chacal, porc-épic, très rare gazelle, gerenuk ou gazelle-giraffe (?), oryctérope (?) pour les mammifères. Des crocodiles sont présents dans le lac ainsi que des hippopotames. La réserve nationale de Sibiloi, à l'est du lac contient aussi des zèbres de Grévy, et l'avifaune est abondante de part et d'autre (Williams, 1981 : 91). La végétation est essentiellement constituée de végétaux xérophiles dont de nombreuses Mimosacées (*Acacia sp.*) et Euphorbiacées, ainsi que quelques Palmacées (*Hyphaene*).

Le climat est aride (moins de 400 mm de pluie par an) et le paysage est semi-désertique en particulier dans la zone d'étude, dans le Rift. Il y a beaucoup de terre érodée («badlands») constitué d'affleurements plio-pléistocènes

---

[1] Nos longs clous de fouilles utilisés pour les carroyages étaient d'ailleurs particulièrement appréciés et justement dérobés régulièrement.

d'argiles, de limons ou de bancs gréseux, entrecoupés de coulées volcaniques subsistant sous forme de plateaux plus ou moins ravinés. De nombreuses roches d'origine volcanique (basalte, trachytes, rhyolithes,...) sont facilement disponibles dans le paysage. Les ressources naturelles sont donc limitées et l'eau est le facteur le plus déterminant dans le rythme des groupes humains qui possèdent une parfaite connaissance des points d'eau creusés dans le sol des lagas.

Habitats

Entre 1996 et 1998 nous avons observé une quinzaine de sites la plupart abandonnés, parfois depuis longtemps (plusieurs années) ou bien depuis quelques jours ; certains étaient encore habités et nous n'avons généralement effectué que de brèves visites parmi ces groupes. Par ailleurs, de très nombreuses structures existent de manière isolée et peuvent, dans certaines zones (le long des lagas par exemple), former un tissu dense de zones d'activité se superposant/cumulant sur plusieurs centaine de mètres.

Il est possible de distinguer plusieurs lieux de vie en fonction du nombre de huttes et de la densité des vestiges au sol (nombre de foyers, présence ou absence d'ossements, et quantité, restes de noix, éléments de broyage, ...). Il est toutefois possible qu'en raison de conditions taphonomiques certains des sites les plus denses ne soit plus reconnaissables en tant que tels (ou créent des palimpsestes). Nous avons alors essayé de relever des sites qui paraissaient les moins dégradés. Nos informations reposent également sur des observations de séjours actuels des groupes dans telles ou telles zones topographiques.

Les sites les plus étendus, regroupant généralement au moins deux familles, constitueraient des lieux de séjour «permanent», avec des durées se déroulant sur une saison ou plus (Type A). Ils sont généralement proches des principaux affluents. De même, dans ces zones assez planes se trouvent des sites plus spécifiques, depuis des arrêts lors de déplacements et de stations pour les troupeaux (Type B) ou en relation plus étroite avec les 'campements' de type A (lieux cérémoniels, activité alimentaire ponctuelle[2], etc.). Des sites, composés de nombreux enclos et de rares huttes sans structure associée, sont localisés plus en hauteur, souvent à mi-pente ; ils représentent des lieux axés sur la garde et le soin de bétail, surtout des ovicaprinés (Type C). Ces sites 'pastoralistes', pouvant avoir une certaine durée d'occupation, sont moins évidents plus bas et se mélangent avec les campements. Enfin, des sites de courte durée, notamment liés à des déplacements ou à des séjours plus spécifiques se placent souvent sur des hauteurs (parfois bien placés, avec de la vue) (Type D). Enfin d'autres zones d'occupation, très ponctuelles sont en relation avec des aires de jeux ou de boucherie par exemple. La densité des gisements va ainsi en décroissant depuis les bas de vallées jusqu'aux hauteurs. Cet étagement pourrait être différent dans d'autres biotopes (hauts plateaux).

Parmi les relevés effectués, les sites les plus importants fournissent des modèles d'occupation récurrente. Les campements réunissent un ensemble de vestiges au sol et de nombreuses structures de fonctions différenciées. Elles réunissent généralement plusieurs familles. Les zones de repos et de séjour spécifique sont des huttes circulaires constituées de branches d'épineux regroupés et liés entre elles, recouverts de branches avec des feuilles plus vertes et également de peaux. Elles ont une forme de dôme géodésique et peuvent avoir jusqu'à 12 m^2 pour une hauteur d'environ 1,60 m. Ces structures se retrouvent chez de nombreuses cultures dans des environnements divers de forêt dense au semi-désert ; elles semblent assez caractéristiques des peuples nomades, accompagnées de structure semi-circulaire (Binford cité par Gamble, 1991 : tabl. 1).

Les huttes et les zones d'activités (en terme de vestiges au sol) associées s'organisent souvent de façon circulaire avec une hutte, un auvent adjacent avec un important foyer (primaire) et au moins un, voire deux, coupe-vent ou petit abri en face de l'entrée principale de la hutte (fig. 1). Il existe plusieurs foyers secondaires. La disposition générale dans certains cas peut être plus linéaire et elle est alors plus simple (moins de structures). Des zones de repos et des zones de consommation sont attestées dans les abords immédiats. Des enclos, riche en fumier et entouré d'épineux se distribuent en périphérie, isolant les plus grosses huttes.

Sans entrer dans le détail d'une description des types (structuration) et nature des occupations (durée, nombre d'individus, activités,...), ou des caractéristiques archéozoologiques des assemblages osseux (techniques de fracturation, marques, etc.), c'est lors de ces relevés que nous avons également remarqué des zones plus denses de vestiges lithiques (fig. 2). Ces concentrations sont parfois associées à des restes osseux, et se trouvent relativement éloignés (20-100 m) des zones d'habitats *s.s.* (huttes+ auvent+ abri/coupe-vent). D'autres restes lithiques se trouvent disséminés, notamment dans les zones proches des lagas ('terrasse inférieure'). Une première description typo-technologique sera donnée ci-dessous permettant d'appréhender les systèmes employés et les sélections opérées de la part des Turkana.

LES ENSEMBLES LITHIQUES

La découverte, dans le contexte décrit précédemment, de matériel lithique totalement dépourvu de patine nous a permis de soupçonner l'utilisation d'outils en pierre par les Turkana. Cette utilisation nous a été confirmée de manière définitive par certains de nos collaborateurs Turkana, démonstration à l'appui.

L'un des éléments les plus novateurs et les plus surprenants, notamment pour un préhistorien expérimentateur, est l'emploi d'une technique de taille tout à fait particulière : la percussion directe d'un nucléus mobile, tenu en main droite, sur un percuteur « dormant », passif, plus ou moins immobile, tenu en main gauche. L'emploi de cette technique n'a, à notre connaissance,

---

[2] Nous avons eu l'occasion d'observer et de suivre intégralement une chasse d'un porc-épic qui a été rapidement par la suite rôti et mangé ; une partie des membres a été ramenée dans un campement proche.

L'outillage lithique en contextes ethnoarchéologiques / Lithic Toolkits in Ethnoarchaeological Contexts

Figure 1. Hutte et abri, foyers, camp de Nayena Engol -1996, (cliché J.P. Brugal)

Figure 2. Zone de concentration de vestiges lithiques, camp de Nayena Engol 55A - 1998, (cliché J.P.Brugal)

jamais été évoquée à ce jour dans le cadre d'un débitage. Tout au plus a-t-elle été mentionnée par certains expérimentateurs comme technique de retouche éventuelle (Inizan *et al.*, 1995). Cette technique est celle qui a été employée spontanément et indépendamment par deux informateurs lorsque nous leur avons demandé de nous confirmer la pratique actuelle de la taille des roches dures.

Les matériaux utilisés relèvent tous de la famille des roches magmatiques, plus particulièrement des roches volcaniques à structure microlitique (rhyolites, basaltes, etc.). Quelques roches métamorphiques ont semble-t-il également été mises à profit malgré les discontinuités que peuvent constituer les plans de schistosité.

Il s'agit dans tous les cas de matériaux relativement ubiquistes, dont l'acquisition peut être considérée comme locale ; cette acquisition n'a donc pas fait l'objet de démarche particulière, si ce n'est peut-être une sélection traduisant une certaine connaissance empirique des matériaux isotropes disponibles.

Une fois que la présence d'outils de pierre par les Turkana a été remarquée, nous en avons trouvé pratiquement dans tous leurs lieux d'occupation ; il faut cependant rester prudent compte tenu de la richesse archéologique de la région considérée. C'est ainsi que nous avons écarté un certain nombre d'éclats, à la fois patinés et émoussés, bien qu'ils aient été découverts au sein de zones d'activités sub-actuelles.

Les pièces qui suivent, en revanche, sont totalement dépourvues de patine et sont généralement concentrées sur un espace réduit. Leur fraîcheur et la présence de remontages permettent de les associer de manière définitive aux activités actuelles des Turkana. Elles ont été recueillies en périphérie d'habitats abandonnés (Type A et C) et leur répartition au sol traduisait une activité humaine relativement récente (répartition non aléatoire par groupes d'objets, présence de remontages à faible distance, etc.). Ces éléments étaient associés à des ossements de chèvres ainsi qu'à de gros blocs portant des traces d'impacts trahissant probablement une utilisation comme percuteur dormant et/ou comme enclume. Nous nous contenterons dans cette note de décrire les vestiges lithiques, sans préciser leurs lieux précis de découvertes et leurs relations avec d'autres vestiges et structures.

Éclats

• *63 x 52 x 15 mm – 56 g – a= 116°*
petit éclat de basalte à talon lisse, à face supérieure partiellement « corticale », probablement débité « sur percuteur dormant mobile ».
Le tranchant droit présente un émoussé d'utilisation très prononcé, observable à l'œil nu, évoquant le travail d'un matériau souple tel que la peau.

• *93 x 70 x 20 mm – 142 g – a = ?*
fragment mésial d'éclat à face supérieure corticale.
Les fractures distales pourraient être volontaires. La technique de débitage reste difficile à préciser en l'absence de partie proximale ; la portion de face inférieure observable est très plane et les stigmates qu'elle comporte évoquent une fracture « en split » relativement violente. La percussion sur percuteur dormant (fixe ou mobile) n'est pas exclue.

• *126 x 101 x 42 mm – 531 g – a =?*
fragment distal d'éclat ou éclat obtenu par « arrachement », avec dans ce cas un talon très déversé (a > 130 °) ; présence de négatifs d'enlèvements antérieurs sur la face supérieure, à l'exception d'une plage corticale centrale.
Pièce massive présentant quelques esquillements pouvant évoquer une utilisation sur son tranchant droit, resté toutefois brut de débitage.

Éclat repris (fig. 3)

total : *134 x 99 x 35 mm – 542 g – a =135°*
éclat seul : *125 x 99 x 35 mm – 452 g – 40 < a tr < 50°*
ensemble de 6 pièces correspondant à un gros éclat transformé en outil, ainsi que les éclats correspondant à l'amincissement de sa partie proximale, sur sa face supérieure.
Le support a très probablement été obtenu par percussion sur un percuteur dormant, sans doute immobile au sol compte tenu de son module.

Bien que les éclats d'amincissement n'interviennent pas sur la face inférieure, il est fort probable qu'ils aient été réalisés après le débitage du support, et ce pour différentes raisons :

- le nucléus dont est issu le support ne se trouvait visiblement pas dans l'espace domestique dont sont issues les pièces considérées : si les éclats remontés sur la face supérieure avaient été débités avant la production du support, ils seraient restés auprès du nucléus (sans préjuger de la distance parcourue par le support).

- si les éclats remontés sur la face supérieure avaient été débités avant la production du support, la partie proximale aurait été trop fine pour transmettre l'énergie importante générée par la percussion sur percuteur dormant et l'opération se serait sans doute soldée par un réfléchissement.

Il convient de noter que ces éclats d'amincissement se sont tous soldés par des réfléchissements ; ceci peut être interprété par une appréciation incorrecte de l'énergie requise pour détacher de tels éclats. Toutefois ces accidents ne semblent pas avoir interdit l'utilisation, comme en témoignent les nombreux esquillements liés à la retouche et/ou l'utilisation sur le tranchant distal. La position de cette partie vraisemblablement active, ainsi que deux petits enlèvements inverses, plaident en faveur de l'aménagement de la partie proximale pour faciliter la préhension.

Bloc façonné (fig. 4)

134 x 135 x 55 mm – 1270 g – a tr > 60°
bloc massif présentant un tranchant sub-rectiligne façonné bifacialement, par une génération d'enlèvement sur une face, par plusieurs sur l'autre.
L'objet en question renvoie à la notion typologique de « chopping-tool » ou de « galet taillé sur deux faces » (même si en l'occurrence le support de départ n'est pas un galet...). La technique de façonnage exclusive est la percussion directe au percuteur dur.

Fragment de plaquette repris

total : *153 x 100 x 35 mm – 825 g*
seul : *128 x 92 x 33 mm – 385 g – 40 < a tr < 50°*
ensemble de 6 pièces correspondant à une plaquette fragmentée « par flexion » (peut-être sur enclume ?), et dont un des morceaux (au moins) a été transformé en outil par retouche.
Le support présente des négatifs antérieurs fortement patinés. Le principal outil identifié dans ce groupe a été retouché bifacialement sur l'un de ses bords par percussion directe au percuteur dur. La retouche est irrégulière en délinéation, en profil comme en plan. La forme de l'objet est globalement symétrique, mais il semble s'agir d'un trait purement conjoncturel et non du résultat d'une recherche spécifique.

Schémas de production

Les *schémas* mis en oeuvre sont relativement simples : ils se résument généralement à l'obtention d'un support présentant un tranchant et éventuellement à la transformation de son tranchant par retouche. Dans un seul cas, une étape supplémentaire est attestée : il s'agit de la retouche de la partie proximale d'un éclat en vue de son amincissement (fig. 5).

Les *méthodes* d'obtention des supports sont extrêmement élémentaires : débitage d'éclats corticaux à partir de blocs non configurés, fractionnement de plaquettes naturelles ou,

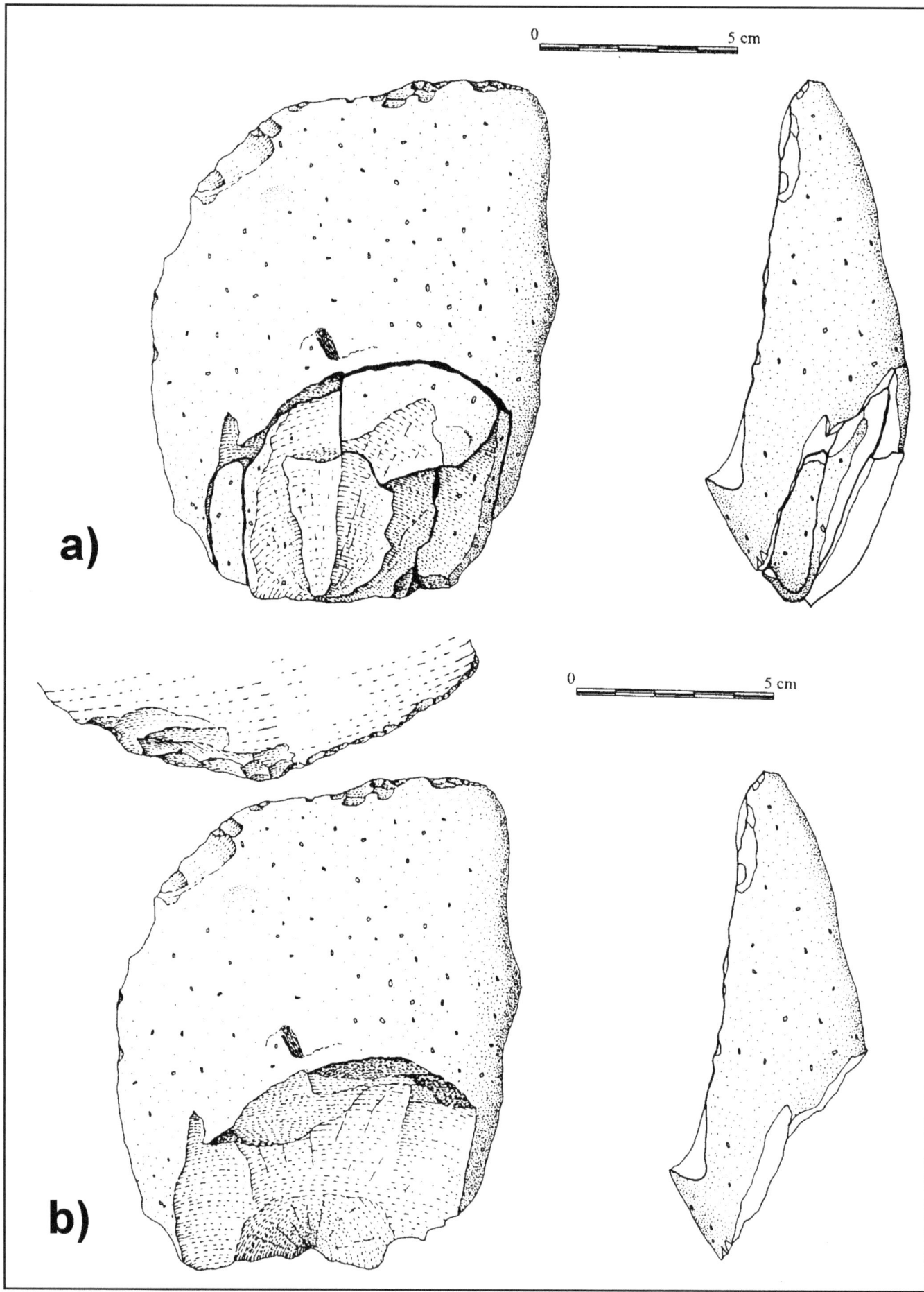

Figure 3. Éclat repris, roche volcanique: a = avec éclats d'amincissement remontés ; b = sans les éclats d'amincissement, (dessin V.Mourre)

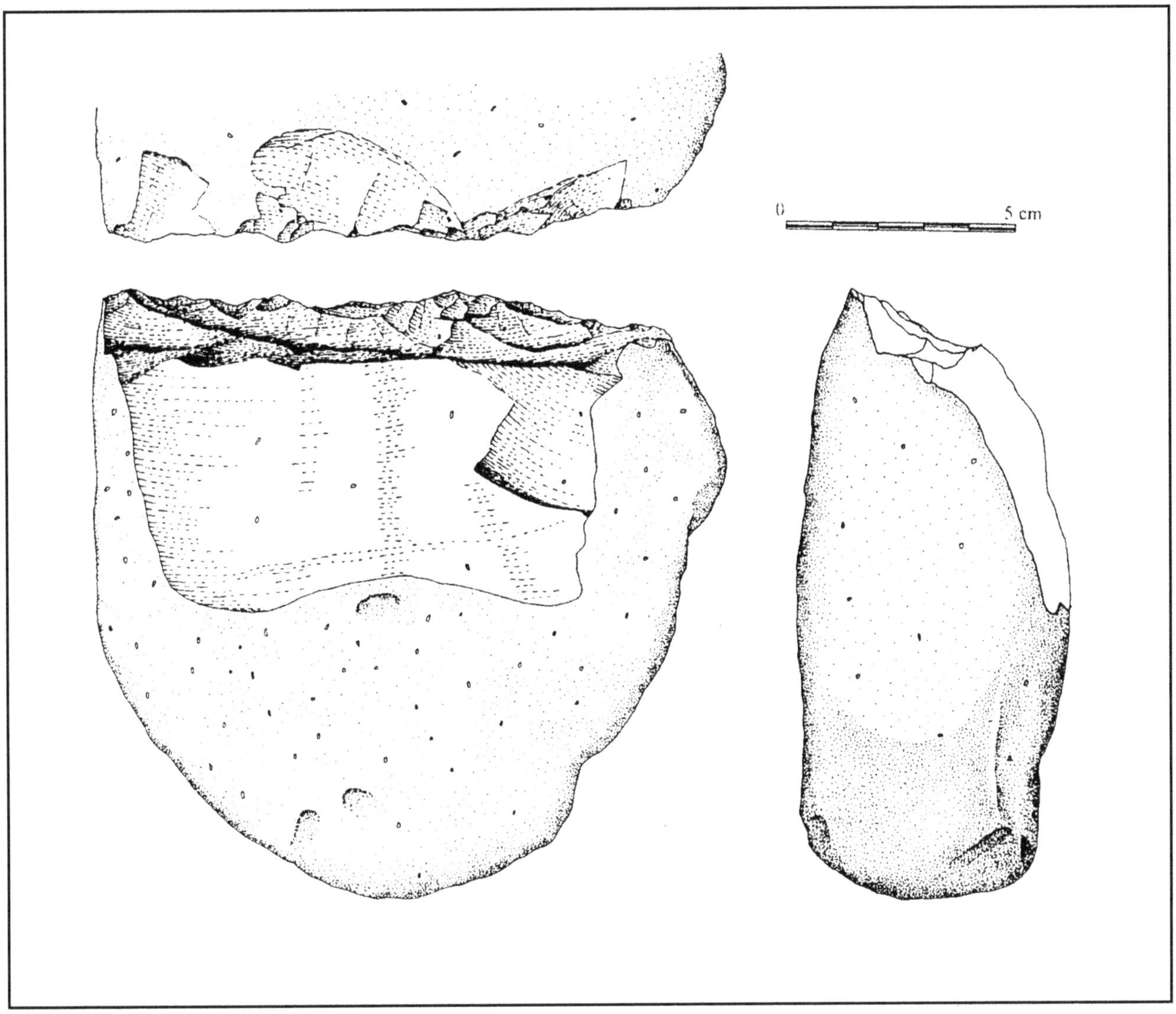

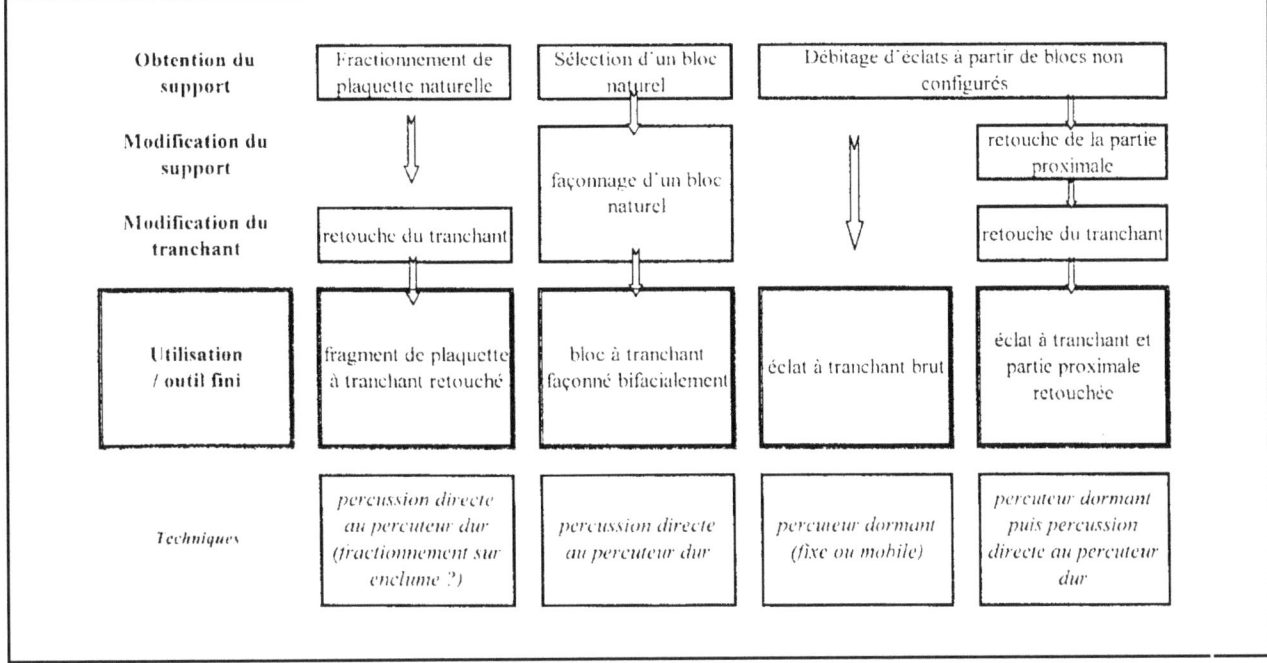

Figure 4. Bloc façonné, roche volcanique (dessin V. Mourre).

Figure 5. Présentation synthétique des schémas de production mis en oeuvre.

tout simplement, sélection de blocs naturels en vue d'un façonnage de type « galet taillé ».

Les *techniques* employées font toutes appel à la percussion dure, même si ses modalités d'application sont relativement diversifiées :

- percussion sur enclume pour le fractionnement de plaquettes,

- percussion sur percuteur dormant (fixe ou mobile) pour le débitage d'éclats,

- percussion directe dure « classique » pour la retouche.

D'après les informations orales et les observations réalisées, l'*utilisation* de ces outils de pierre semble généralement liée à la consommation d'aliment (dépeçage/découpe de viande, fracturation des os pour consommer la moelle, etc.). Dans ce cas, la durée d'utilisation semble assez limitée et les outils sont abandonnés immédiatement. Mais il faut rappeler aussi l'existence d'un éclat ayant probablement été utilisé pour le travail de la peau jusqu'à présenter un émoussé visible à l'œil nu : il se pourrait donc que des outils particulièrement adaptés soient conservés un certain temps. Quoi qu'il en soit, l'utilisation de pierres taillées reste extrêmement opportuniste, en ce sens que les outils sont produits suivant des schémas simples, pour la satisfaction d'un besoin immédiat et hors de toute notion d'anticipation.

Avant de conclure, il convient de préciser le rapport qu'entretiennent les Turkana actuels avec le métal : ces pasteurs-nomades connaissent le métal et l'utilisent, notamment sous la forme de couteaux-bracelets très caractéristiques portés par les hommes. Cependant, ils ne maîtrisent pas sa production et l'obtiennent par échanges avec des groupes voisins plus ou moins éloignés : ainsi, dès la fin du XIXème siècle, le trafic d'ivoire avec l'Éthiopie a permis le développement du commerce de l'étain et du cuivre, destinés à la parure, tandis que le fer était importé d'Ouganda par l'intermédiaire des Jie, un autre groupe nilotique proche des Turkana (Pavitt, 1997). La fin du commerce de l'ivoire, suite à l'extermination des éléphants dans la région, et la création de centres urbains par l'administration britannique ont bien sûr modifié les sources d'approvisionnement en métal.

Les Turkana ne disposent que de techniques de transformation élémentaires et travaillent apparemment les métaux par martelage sans chauffe. Si cette technique donne de bons résultats pour le cuivre et l'étain, très malléables, elle est plus aléatoire pour le fer. Il est donc vraisemblable que les objets les plus élaborés, tels que les couteaux-bracelets des adultes, soient acquis sous leur forme définitive. Mais la transformation du fer par martelage à froid est aussi pratiquée ponctuellement. Nous avons observé directement l'utilisation de ce type de martelage à froid entre deux petits galets de quartz pour l'affûtage d'une lame de couteau emmanché. D'autre part, nous avons aussi pu observer à différentes reprises des couteaux-bracelets grossiers, portés par des enfants Turkana : ces couteaux étaient visiblement produits par martelage à partir de clous par exemple. Les Turkana se trouvent donc en situation de dépendance vis-à-vis de l'approvisionnement en métaux et de leur transformation en objets élaborés. Il est donc tout à fait logique qu'ils aient eu, à un moment ou à un autre, la nécessité et/ou le désir de leur substituer des matériaux disponibles dans leur environnement et dont ils maîtrisaient la transformation.

CONCLUSION

Les Turkana habitent une région aride et leurs environnements (plaines et piedmont d'escarpements du Rift, hauts plateaux) peuvent être qualifiés de difficile en terme de ressources (en particulier en eau et pâturages), expliquant en partie leur grande mobilité. Cette mobilité pourrait peut-être expliquer leur relatif dénuement matériel. L'étude des campements et des structures est riche d'informations car présentant un champ analogique à la fois socio-économique mais aussi taphonomique. Il s'agit d'une démarche actualiste, commune à l'ethnoarchéologie, par laquelle sont favorisées les distributions spatiales intra- et inter-sites, avec la présence-absence et les concentrations de vestiges, leurs relations exprimées en terme d'association et/ou d'exclusion. L'implantation et l'importance des habitats définissent un tissu d'occupations et d'activités en accord avec les données sur les modes de vie actuels. A ce niveau, la comparaison avec des modèles d'installation décrits chez les chasseurs-cueilleurs peut être envisagée (cf. Panter-Brick et al, 2001 pour une introduction sur la notion de chasseur-cueilleur). Il est également possible d'appréhender les processus de formation des sites mais surtout de leurs processus de destruction et de désorganisation. Dans ce cadre nous avons alors opté pour une approche archéologique (relevés) pour interpréter les données résiduelles d'un campement. Les vestiges lithiques et osseux, les restes périssables (bois, noix, tissu…) et les structures en pierres (foyer, «table» de boucherie, etc.), les éléments structurants (arbre, point d'eau, etc.) sont autant de facteurs pris en compte dans la compréhension de l'organisation spatiale des activités.

Dans cette note, nous nous sommes restreints à la présentation des ensembles lithiques associés à des habitats de différente nature (campements, haltes, etc.). La découverte de l'utilisation ponctuelle d'outils de pierre taillée par les Turkana est intéressante à plusieurs titres. Elle montre avant tout qu'il est possible de produire un outillage diversifié en ne mettant en œuvre que des méthodes et des techniques élémentaires. Elle nous a permis aussi d'identifier l'emploi d'une technique jusqu'ici non décrite, la percussion directe d'un nucléus sur un percuteur « dormant », passif mais tenu en main. Ses possibilités restent à explorer par l'expérimentation pour d'éventuelles confrontations avec le matériel archéologique. L'histoire de cette technique en particulier et de l'utilisation d'outils de pierre par les Turkana en général semble malheureusement bien difficile à déterminer. En effet, il sera délicat d'établir si nous avons affaire à la persistance ou à la redécouverte d'un comportement ancestral. Enfin, cette découverte confirme si besoin était – que les pasteurs-nomades Turkana détiennent d'extraordinaires capacités d'adaptation à un environnement semi-désertique extrêmement rude.

Adresses des auteurs

Jean-Philip BRUGAL
Maison Méditerranéenne des Sciences de l'Homme
UMR 6636 BP647
13094 F-Aix-en-Provence FRANCE
Email : brugal@mmsh.univ-aix.fr

Vincent MOURRE
Maison de l'Archéologie et de l'Ethnologie
UPR 7549
21 allée de l'Université
92023 F-Nanterre cedex FRANCE et
Les Hauts Arthèmes
F-84560 Ménerbes FRANCE
Email : vincent.mourre@wanadoo.fr

Remerciements

Tous nos remerciements au *West Turkana Archaeological Project* dirigé par H.Roche et M.Kibunjia, et au Min. français des Affaires Etrangères, qui nous permettent de travailler dans cette superbe région. Merci à tous les Turkana qui nous accueillent avec tant de générosité.

Bibliographie

ADAMSON J., 1967. *The peoples of Kenya*. London : Collins and Harvill Press.

AMIN M., 1981. Cradle of Mankind. Nairobi : Camerapix Publ. Intern., 191 p.

FEDDERS A., SALVADORI C., 1989 (4é éd.). Peoples and Cultures of Kenya, Nairobi : Transafrica et London : Rex Collings, 164 p.

GAMBLE C., 1991. An introduction to the living spaces of mobile peoples. In *Ethnoarchaeological approaches to mobile campsites*, C.S.Gamble, W.A.Boismier (eds.), International Monographs in Prehistory, Ethnoarch.Ser. 1 : p. 1-23.

INIZAN M-L., REDURON-BALLINGER M., ROCHE, H., TIXIER, J., 1995. *Préhistoire de la pierre taillée t. 4 - Technologie de la pierre taillée*. Meudon : CREP, 199 p.

JONES D.K., 1984. Shepherds of the Desert. London : Elm Tree Books, 184 p.

KENT S., 1991. The relationship between mobility strategies and site structure. In *The Interpretation of archaeological spatial patterning*, E.M.Kroll, T.D.Price (eds.), New York & London : Plenum Press, p; 33-59.

LEAKEY R.E., 1981. *The Making of Mankind*. London : Michael Joseph Limited, 256 p.

LEAKEY R., LEWIN R. 1979. *Peoples of the Lake*. London : Collins et New York : Doubleday.

LEAKEY R., LEWIN R. 1985. *Les origines de l'Homme*. Paris : Flammarion, 280 p.

NOAD T., BIRNIE A. (eds.), 1989. *Trees of Kenya*. Nairobi, 308 p.

PANTER-BRICK C., LAYTON R.H., ROWLEY-CONWY P. (eds.), 2001. Lines of Enquiry. In *Hunter-Gathrerer, an interdisciplinary perspective*. Cambridge University Press, p. 1-11.

PAVITT N., 1997. *Turkana, nomads of the Jade Sea*. London : Harvill Press, 240 p.

ROCHE H., DELAGNES A., BRUGAL J.P., FEIBEL C., KIBUNJIA M., MOURRE V., TEXIER P.J., 1999. Early hominid stone tool production and technical skill 2.34 Myr ago, in West Turkana, Kenya. *Nature*, 6731 : p. 57-60.

WILLIANS J.G., 1981 (2nd ed.). *A field guide to the National Parks of East Africa*. London : Collins, 336 p.

REVERSE KNAPPING IN THE ANTIPODES: THE SPATIAL IMPLICATIONS OF ALTERNATE APPROACHES TO KNAPPING

Peter HISCOCK

Résumé : Des observations sur les Aborigènes australiens qui travaillent la pierre ont fréquemment suggéré des principes d'analyse différents de ceux qui sont classiques. L'un des observateurs les mieux connus, Brian Hayden (1977), a constaté que les activités de ces Aborigènes qui travaillent la pierre nous ont fourni quelques « surprises ». Ces « surprises » ont constitué un défi aux interprétations traditionnelles des styles et des fonctions des outils en pierre. La communication présente développe ce point de vue, en rapportant des observations, faites pendant les années soixante-dix, sur deux vieillards Alyawerre (Alyawara) d'Australie centrale. Des aspects de la manière dont ces hommes ont fait craquer la pierre, et des caractéristiques spatiales des débris archéologiques qui en ont résulté, sont décrits dans cette communication. Les activités de ces travailleurs illustrent un système « inverse » de faire craquer la pierre. C'est un système qui normalement n'est pas considéré dans les interprétations archéologiques, et il souligne la nécessité pour les archéologues de favoriser la recherche de modèles divers du passé.

Abstract: Observations of Australian Aboriginals working stone have often suggested alternatives to conventional principles used in archaeological analyses. One of the most well-known observers, Brian Hayden (1977), noted that the activities of Aboriginal knapper's provided a number of 'surprises' that constituted a challenge to common stylistic and functional interpretations of stone implements. This paper develops this viewpoint by reporting on observations, made in the 1970's, of two old Alyawerre (Alyawara) men from Central Australia. Aspects of the knapping procedures of these men, and the spatial patterning of the archaeological debris, are described. The activities of these stoneworkers illustrate a 'reverse' system of knapping that is not normally considered in archaeological interpretations, and highlights the necessity for archaeologists to seek diverse models of the past.

One of the more productive uses of ethnographic observations is as a test of archaeological principles. In some instances these observations of the contemporary world act as 'spoilers' to refute interpretative principles otherwise presumed to be universally applicable (see Walters 1990). Observations of Australian Aboriginals working stone have on occasion revealed alternatives to conventional principles used in archaeological analyses. Since there is no reason that the kinds of knapping activities observed in Australia were, in the past, restricted to Sahul they represent models which may have value in archaeological interpretations of both the Old and New World. A well-known example of this is Brian Hayden's (1977) report that the activities of Western Desert Aboriginal knapper's provided a number of 'surprises' that constituted a challenge to common stylistic and functional interpretations of stone implements (see also Hiscock 1998). This paper describes another example of Aboriginal knapping from the Australian desert that has implications for interpretation of knapping areas identified in archaeological sites. The author made these observations between 11-13 September 1978. This period was spent with Slippery Morton and Billy Dempsey, who were then old men, *Alyawerre* (Alyawarra) speakers from Amaroo, in Central Australian. Slippery and Billy were old enough to have been exposed to traditional (ie. at least pre-twentieth century) practices of stone knapping, and these practices had being demonstrated to Slippery and Billy when they were young men at the start of the twentieth century. Their knapping was performed with a distinctive twisting motion that struck flakes behind the knapper; a system that can loosely be termed *reverse knapping*.

SLIPPERY AND BILLY KNAPPING

The lithic material they used to make these artefacts was a uniformly grained white and light grey quartzite occurring as rounded nodules encased in a soft orange cortex often several centimetres thick. These rocks naturally crop out in a variety of sizes: from pieces weighing only 800 grams up to large boulders which are usually broken down by fire cracking and pounding with other large rocks. A variety of quartzite hammerstones of various sizes were used, the smallest weighed 576 grams.

Over a two-day period Slippery and Billy spent six hours knapping stone. Further time was spent preparing resin. The outcome of this labour was the production of 12 stone knives set in resin handles. These objects were said to function as 'knives', with a strong, gradually curving circular or semi-circular edge. In size the knives varied from 6 cm to15 cm, and shapes varied from circular to elongate with circular distal ends. All of the 'knives' were sold.

Flakes were struck from large, typically bifacial cores. Much of the preparatory knapping involved stripping the thick orange cortex from the core. The main obstacle to continued reduction was the production of large step terminated scars on the core face. Cores were usually reduced until thoroughly exhausted.

In 1978 Billy Dempsey did all of the knapping. At that time Slippery was somewhat subdued because of a recent coronary and left most of the active roles to Billy.

Slippery's incapacity may have modified their behaviour, but the activities I observed were virtually identical with the previously filmed knapping of these men. This knapping involved twisting, cross-body percussion blows to the cores.

The typical knapping posture for Billy was kneeling on the ground. The core rested on the ground to the left and front of Billy's left knee, between 0.3 and 0.8 of a metre from his body (see Figure 1). This core was positioned and manipulated by Billy's left hand. The hammerstone was held in his right hand. In the act of knapping Billy would bring the right hand round in an arc and down toward his left kidney, hitting the uppermost part of the core by his left knee.

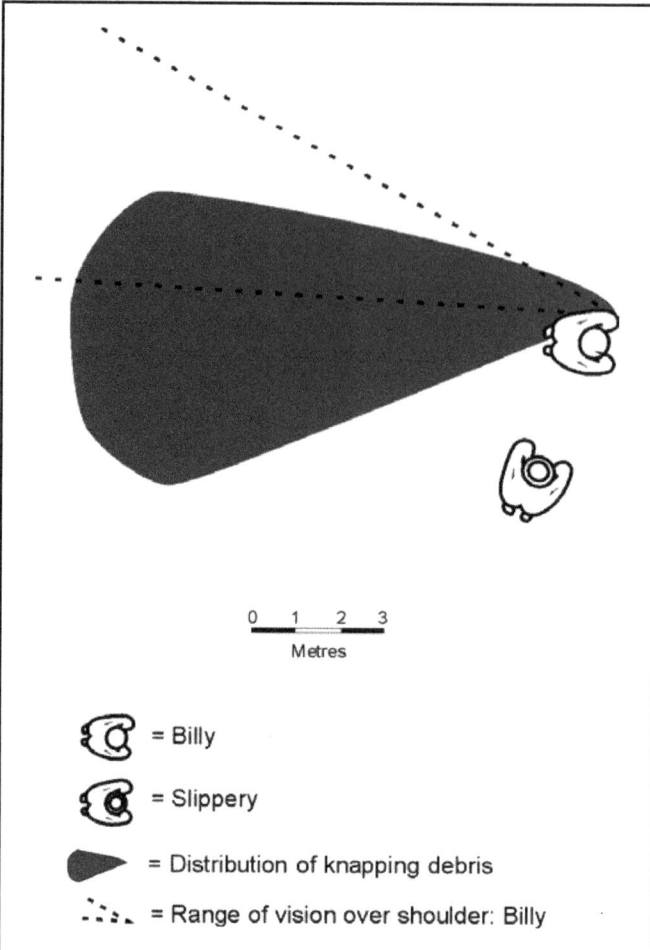

Figure 2. A depiction of the spatial distribution of knapping debris in unvegetated areas.

Figure 1. Illustration of the body position of Billy Dempsey while knapping.

Successfully detached flakes would fly to the left and behind the knapper, hence the description of this as 'reverse knapping'. Figure 2 shows schematically the spatial relationship between Billy, the scatter of flakes he produced, and his field of vision when seated. This approach to knapping created an elongated cone-shaped distribution of artefacts behind the knapper. Detached flakes landed out of Billy's sight and anywhere from centimetres to twelve metres from his back. The highest density of material was found within four metres of the knapper. On occasions when Billy sat away from large plants flakes up to 8cm long landed metres from the core and showed no ill effects from their journey.

This extended scatter behind the knapper was only produced when Billy sat in clear areas. Sometimes Billy chose to sit in front of large and tall clumps of grass. As the knapper struck flakes, they would fly into, and be trapped by, the stands of grass. This strategy minimised inconvenience when retrieving specimens by restricting the area of debris to a few square metres. As a result, the same knapping procedure could create a small or elongated scatter of debris behind the knapper, the size and shape of the knapping debris being largely determined by the position of the knapper in relation to objects such as rock and vegetation that could act as a barrier to the flight of flakes struck from the cores.

One consequence of this twisting cross-body reverse knapping action was that much of the flaking debris accumulated at the rear of the knapper, and could not be viewed by the knapper. Because Billy was unable to observe flakes he struck off it was his habit to have an aid, in this case his friend Slippery. Slippery looked at the flakes that had been detached behind Billy's back and retrieved some for closer inspection. Slippery sat to the right of the knapper and parallel to, or slightly behind him (see Figure 2). In that way Slippery was protected from any airborne flakes, but he remained some distance from the landing flakes; and on occasions where he was not far behind the knapper he also had to twist his torso to examine the knapping results. This created the intriguing circumstance in which a knapper was often unaware of the flakes that were produced, and the identification of flakes suitable for use was made by someone other than the knapper. The consequence of this will be examined on another occasion. What is worth noting here is that this reverse knapping is not restricted to any one areas or group of people in Australia.

A SECOND ETHNOGRAPHIC EXAMPLE

It is worth noting that similar body positions and approaches to knapping have been observed widely in Australia. For example, Jones and White (1988:65) published photographs of Diltjima, a senior Marra-larr-mirri man knapping quartzite blocks in 1981 at a small quarry near Ngilipitji in eastern Arnhem Land. (This region is more than 1500 km distant from the central Australian location of Slippery and Billy). In these photographs Diltjima adopted a semi-seated posture with legs separated, one leg directly under his body the other folded at right angles. Although this superficially contrasts with the kneeling posture of Billy Dempsey, the knapping procedure is otherwise strikingly similar (see Figure 3b). The right-handed Diltjima immobilised the core on the ground with his left hand and swung the hammer in an arc across his body with his right hand to remove flakes beside or behind his left side. Jones and White (1988) describe the cores knapped in this way as generating regular 'blades' from a single platform. Their description of Diltjima's knapping was as follows:

> With his left hand, he secured the core in position, holding its upper surface a few centimetres back from its edge and pressing it slightly down onto the grass pad. He then struck the core with a long sideways and slightly downwards blow which travelled across the front of his body... The point of contact was at his side, with the front of his body still facing parallel to the plane of the core platform. (Jones and White 1988: 62-64)

This description alone is sufficient to indicate that this twisting, across-the-body approach to percussion knapping was employed widely in Australia during the historic period. This conclusion raises the question: "if this is a viable method of striking flakes from cores, when and where was it employed?"

DISCUSSION

This question is significant because the twisting reverse knapping practice differs from the knapping procedure employed by western replicators and used by most archaeologists modelling prehistoric activities (Figure 3). Archaeological interpretations of knapping have conventionally assumed the prehistoric knappers did what modern archaeologists do: sit on a chair (or rock), striking downward with a hammer to remove flakes which fell in front of the knapper, between his/her legs (see Figure 3c). The capacity to distinguish between these two approaches, the 'reverse' and the 'frontal', is important if archaeologists are to infer the position and orientation of ancient knapper's within archaeological sites. Figure 4 illustrates that the twisting approach discussed here can create scatters the range from small and circular to large and elongated, depending on the circumstance; but no matter what the shape of the scatter may be it is positioned to the side and rear of the knapper. This contrasts to the location of debris in front of the seated, western knapper (Figure 4c).

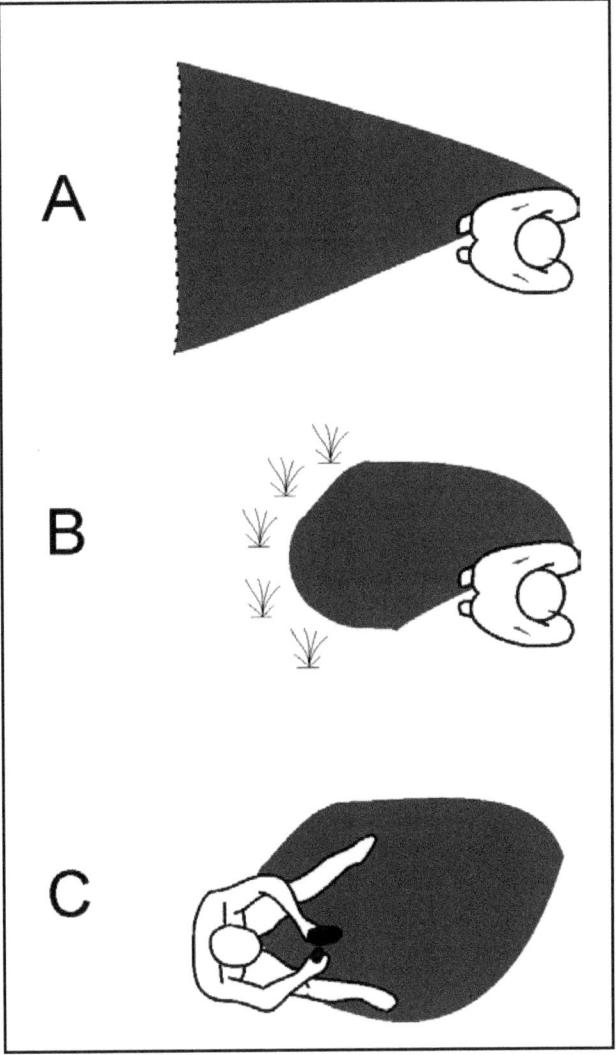

Figure 4. A comparison of the relationship of knapper and knapping debris: a) Slippery and Billy in unvegetated areas, b) Slippery and Billy near barrier vegetation, and c) conventional western approach.

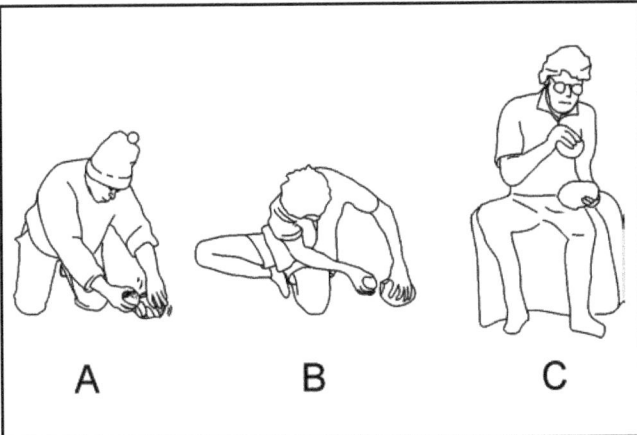

Figure 3. A comparison of the knapping actions of: a) Billy Dempsey, b) Diltjima (after Jones and White 1988), and c) conventional western approach (after Fischer 1990).

In recent decades it has been fashionable to build detailed reconstructions of short moments in prehistoric life, in which the archaeological manufacturing debris is used to interpret the actions of individual artisans, and so archaeologists have discussed where and how the knapper worked within the site. Despite the numerous elaborate and well described studies of the spatial distribution of lithic material in artefact scatters, often aided by extensive conjoining, the interpretations of prehistoric knapping is often built on the seated model of knapping behaviours, which is presumed to be universally applicable. In such a context the existence of alternative models of knapping behaviour, such as the reverse knapping described here, creates a challenge to archaeologists to avoid ethnocentric assumptions when modelling artefact manufacture.

A short commentary on some European interpretations of knapping floors can illustrate the common assumption of frontal body positions and the potential of reverse knapping to create similar archaeological patterns. Many artefact scatters that have been interpreted as knapping floors covered are 1-8 metres in length (eg. Bergman et al 1990; Collcut, Barton, and Bergman 1990; Cziesla 1990; Fischer 1990; Gilead and Fabian 1990; Roeboeks and Hennekens 1990; Schon 1990; Weiner 1990; Ziesaire 1990). Knapping floors of this size could have been created either by frontal or reverse knapping, but have normally been explicitly interpreted as a product of frontal flaking. This explanation has been bolstered at some sites where structural features have been interpreted in terms of a frontal model of flaking. For example, when blocks of stone have been found in or on the edge of knapping floors they have often been interpreted as 'seats' for the knapper (eg. Fischer 1990; Weiner 1990), although one plausible alternative is that these objects are barriers to the flight of flakes in reverse knapping, in which the knapper knelt on the ground facing away from the rock. Reverse knapping could be invoked to explain elongated rather than circular shaped knapping floors that some researchers have noted (eg. Roeboeks and Hennekens 1990), single outlying flakes a few metres outside the cluster of artefacts forming a knapping floor, or even the cone-shaped distribution of refitting sequences that have cores positioned at the apex of the cone, as documented by Gilead and Fabian (1990). Even the discovery of conjoined flakes even 10-15 metres from the core need not indicate that people carried flakes from the knapping floor to a second locality. Indeed, many of the features of Old World archaeological knapping floors may be explicable as the product of either frontal or reverse knapping. It is not the purpose of this paper to suggest what method of knapping took place at any particular locality. Rather, the point is that the archaeological patterns could conceivably be produced by a knapping approach other than the frontal model that is traditionally applied, and interpretations have often not considered plausible alternatives such as those revealed in ethnographic descriptions.

Differentiating the archaeological signatures of frontal or reverse systems of knapping may require more detailed information than simply characteristics such as scatter size and the presence of large rocks. The distribution of flake size, and even microdebitage density across an artefact scatter may be the sort of evidence that is required to distinguish the most appropriate model in a specific instance. Experimental trials will probably be necessary to define the principles relevant to such studies. Given the ethnographic observations of different approaches to percussion knapping the claims of archaeologists to have identified the location and orientation of prehistoric knappers may suffer problems of equifinality if detailed measurements of archaeological knapping floors, grounded in experiments, are not made.

CONCLUSION

There is no single approach to percussion knapping, and consequently there is no single spatial association between a knapper and the position and shape of the scatter of debris resulting from knapping. The reverse knapping methods documented here reveals that some approaches to knapping create a concentration behind rather than to the front of the knapper. The existence of an alternative way of striking flakes from a core may be described as yet another 'surprise' deriving from observations of Australian Aboriginal knappers. The implications of observations such as the one reported here must be incorporated into archaeological studies if our interpretations of prehistoric knapping are to be robust and well founded. Failure to consider such antipodean alternatives would condemn archaeological interpretations to reproduce only one of a number of possible images of the past; an outcome that could obscure variability in past hominid behaviour.

Author's address

Peter HISCOCK
School of Archaeology and Anthropology,
Australian National University
Canberra, AUSTRALIA

Bibliography

BERGMAN, C.A., M.B. ROBERTS, S. COLLCUT & P. BARLOW, 1990 Refitting and spatial analysis of artefacts from Quarry 2 at the Middle Pleistocene Acheulean site of Boxgrove, West Sussex, England. Pp.265-281 in Cziesla, E., S. Eickhoff, N. Arts, and D. Winter (eds) *The big puzzle. International symposium on refitting stone artefacts*. Holos, Bonn.

COLLCUT, S.N., N.R.E. BARTON & C. BERGMAN 1990 Refitting in context: a taphonomic case study from a late Upper Palaeolithic site in sands on Hengistbury Head, Dorset, Great Britain. Pp.219-235 in Cziesla, E., S.Eickhoff, N. Arts, and D. Winter (eds) *The big puzzle. International symposium on refitting stone artefacts*. Holos, Bonn.

CZIESLA, E. 1990 Artefact production and spatial distribution on the open air site 80/14 (Western Desert, Egypt). Pp.583-610 in Cziesla, E., S. Eickhoff, N. Arts, and D. Winter (eds) *The big puzzle. International symposium on refitting stone artefacts*. Holos, Bonn.

FISCHER, A. 1990 On being a pupil of a flintknapper 11,000 years ago. A preliminary analysis of settlement organisation and flint technology based on conjoined flint artefacts from the Trollesgrave site. Pp.446-464 in Cziesla, E., S. Eickhoff, N. Arts, and D. Winter (eds) *The big puzzle. International symposium on refitting stone artefacts*. Holos, Bonn.

GILEAD, I. & P.FABIAN 1990 Conjoinable artefacts from the Middle Palaeolithic open air site Fara II, northern Negev, Israel: a preliminary report. Pp.101-112 in Cziesla, E., S. Eickhoff, N. Arts, and D. Winter (eds) *The big puzzle. International symposium on refitting stone artefacts*. Holos, Bonn.

HAYDEN, B. 1977 Stone tool functions in the Western Desert, pp. 178-188 in *Stone Tools as Cultural Markers: Change, Evolution and Complexity*, R. V. S. Wright (Ed.), Humanities Press Inc.

HISCOCK, P. 1998 Revitalising artefact analysis. In T. Murray (ed.) *Archaeology of Aboriginal Australia*, pp.257-265. Sydney: Unwin and Allen.

JONES, R. & N. WHITE 1988 Point blank: stone tool manufacture at the Ngilipitji Quarry, Arnhem Land, 1981. Pp. 51-87 in B. Meehan and R. Jones (eds) *Archaeology with ethnography: an Australian perspective*. Highland Press

ROEBOEKS, W. & P.HENNEKENS 1990 Transport of lithics in the Middle Palaeolithic: conjoining evidence from Maastricht-Belvedere (Nabulae Lisa). Pp.283-295 in Cziesla, E., S. Eickhoff, N. Arts, and D. Winter (eds) *The big puzzle. International symposium on refitting stone artefacts*. Holos, Bonn.

SCHON, W. 1990 Two knapping sites from southwest Egypt: a comparison. Pp.507-513 in Cziesla, E., S. Eickhoff, N. Arts, and D. Winter (eds) *The big puzzle. International symposium on refitting stone artefacts*. Holos, Bonn.

WALTERS, I. 1990 The necessary science of taphonomy, Pp. 18-24 in S. Solomon, I. Davidson, and D. Watson (Eds) *Problem solving in Taphonomy: studies related to the Archaeology of Europe, Africa and Oceania*. Tempus monograph 2, University of Queensland.

WEINER, J. 1990 Intra-site analysis by refitting lithic artefacts from a flint-workshop on the Neolithic flint-mine "Lousberg" in Aachen (Northrhine Westfalia, FRG). Pp.177-196 in Cziesla, E., S. Eickhoff, N. Arts, and D. Winter (eds) *The big puzzle. International symposium on refitting stone artefacts*. Holos, Bonn.

ZIESAIRE, P. 1990 Refitting flaking tools from an early Mesolithic site at Altwies-Haed, Grand Duchy of Luxembourg. Pp.253-261 in Cziesla, E., S. Eickhoff, N. Arts, and D. Winter (eds) *The big puzzle. International symposium on refitting stone artefacts*. Holos, Bonn.

THE MANUFACTURE AND USE OF LEATHER CONSUMPTION GOODS BY THE *YAMANA* OF TUNEL VII, NORTHERN COAST OF BEAGLE CHANNEL (ARGENTINA): AN ETHNOGRAPHIC EVALUATION AND ITS ARCHAEOLOGICAL COMPARISION

Ignacio CLEMENTE CONTE

Résumé : Dans ce travail nous avons utilisé les sources écrites des ethnographes, voyageurs et colons qui eurent un contact avec les Yamana (Terre de Feu) avant leur disparition au début du XXème siècle, pour savoir comment ils travaillaient les peaux pour leur conservation et la fabrication de biens de consommations. Nous analysons aussi les outils lithiques récupérés dans les fouilles archéologiques de Tunel VII et à l'aide de l'analyse fonctionnelle, nous caractérisons ceux qui furent utilises dans le travail sur la peau et cuirs, afin de déterminer le mieux possible les activités des différents processus de fabrication dans lesquels ils sont intervenus.

Abstract: In this work we use sources written by ethnographers, travellers and settlers who had contact with the Yamana (Tierra del Fuego) before they disappeared at the beginning of the 20th century, in order to see how they preserved and prepared hides for manufacture. We analyse also the lithic tools recovered from the archaeological excavations of Tunel VII. By functional analysis, we categorise those used for fur and for leather preparation aiming to get a better understanding of different production processes in which such lithic instruments were used.

INTRODUCTION

In this work we will not make an overview of fur and leather goods manufactured and used by the *Yamana*. Such has already been presented in previous works (Clemente, 1996) and all ethno historical sources were meticulously reviewed in one specific publication about the material and social life of the *Yamana* (Orquera y Piana, 1999). However, we shall discuss how fur was treated for its preservation and use according to the written sources, and compare the data from these sources with the activities registered by traces on the surfaces of lithic instruments from the Tunel VII site.

For the manufacture of different consumer goods, the *Yamana* used furs of different animals, according to their purpose (see Roquera and Piana, op. cit.). They used furs of mammals like: **guanaco** (Lama guanicoe), **foxes** (*Canis seu Cerdocyon magellanicus and Canis griseus*), **otter** (*Lutra felina*), *pinnipedia*: southern sea lion (*Otaria flavescens*) and southern fur seal (*Arthocephalus australis*) especially, and occasionally other *pinnipedia* and phocids which can be found in the region, such as **sea lion** (*Mirounga leonina*), sea leopard (*Hydrurga leptonyx*), crabeater seal (*Lobodon carcinophagus*) and Wedell seal (*Leptonichotes wedellii*). In the late period, after the European introduction – other species – such as beaver (*Castor fiber*), rabbit (*Oryctolagus cuniculus*) or sheep (*Ovis aries*). Skins of birds, as penguin (*Speniscus magellanicus, Eudyptes crestatus, Aptenodytes patagonico y Ap. forsteri*) and cormarant (*Phalacrocórax alviventer, Ph. Magellanicus y Ph. olivaceus*) also were used.

The furs were used for the manufacture of products: garments such as short cloaks, sex cover, sandals; wristbands and ankle socks as ornaments; bags, jugs to bail out water from canoes, working gloves or hand protection, quivers for arrows, slings, leather straps, hut covers, etc.

WRITTEN SOURCES ABOUT FUR AND LEATHER TREATMENT

When they wanted to use the skin of the animal (*pinnipedia*, guanaco, otter…) the hunter removed the fur and subcutaneous fat; women were responsible for cleaning away all fat, and muscular and conjunctive fibber adherences, and than lay it on the ground *"well stretched, between short stakes, or on a railings of short sticks"* (Gusinde, 1986). The stakes used for this purpose are also mentioned by T. Bridges (1933) and G.P. Despard (1859).

Based on the data by J. Cooper (1946) and C.S. Coon (1977), M.E. Mansur (1984:289) says that after the extraction of animal skin " *the Yámanas eliminated the fat adhered to the interior surface. After that, the fur was stretched on the ground using sticks, and left to dry for two or three weeks. Once thoroughly dried, the fur was scraped by a sharp edged shell to make it slim, taking off one layer from the subcutaneous side of the hide. They may have added a lubricating substance made of fat and ash. Unfortunately, we can't know at which moment of the treatment it was added. Nevertheless, we suppose that it was in the next stage of kneading and not during the scraping"*.

M. Gusinde (1986) broadens this data assuring that they first left furs to be dried in the open air, usually supported vertically on one of the exterior "walls" of the hut, or stretched on the wooden railings on which the interior part of the fur was leaned.

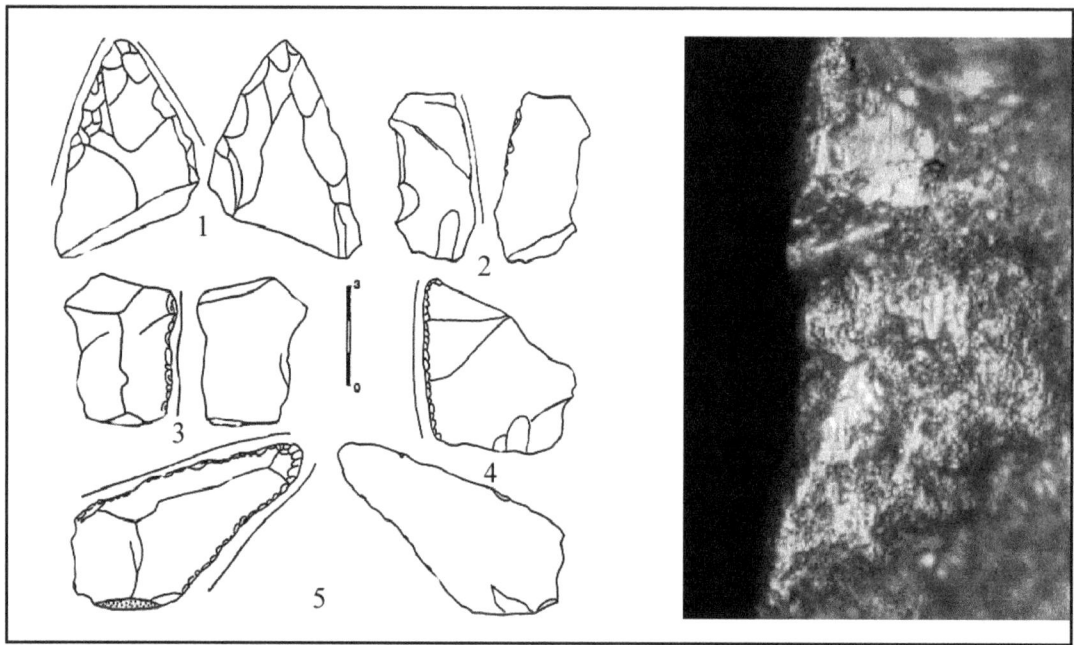

Figure 1. The Tunel VII tools used for skinning animals and/or cutting the fur (left) and microwear polish by this activity -200X- (right).

If the furs were assigned to cover the hut, they didn't require special preparation. When the fur was assigned some other purpose, a woman was responsible for cleaning it by scraping. For certain uses (cloak, sling, etc) the fur had to be depilated (Gusinde, 1986). If the surface to be treated was small, they did it by scraping, or simply pulling out the hair (as in the case of otter). If the surface was big, they usually carried out a putrefaction process (Gusinde, 1986; Hyades y Deniker, 1891)."*In some cases the entire fur was placed under the bed, from where previously a thin layer of earth was removed, and then covered again by humid earth, pasture or moss. Finally, the bed was moved back in its usual place... life in the hut resumes its usual rhythm, without concern. With the humidity from below and a little bit of warmth from above, a kind of fermentation is produced which makes the layer of hair fall off. Finally, it is easy to remove it with the palm, as soon as a sticky and viscous layer covers the leather. There is another procedure in which the women have more success. She spreads her own urine over the piece of fur placed with the hair side up, and leaves it for a while to penetrate, regardless of whether this piece remains several days in the hut or outside, and at the same time it receives soil humidity. People used to consider that human urine is more efficient when immediately after spreading it over the piece of fur it is rubbed by the palm of the hand or with sawdust, while it is still warm. After repeating the procedure several times, the fur is covered by a thin coating of moist earth, and she frequently sits on it, or lies down to sleep, transmitting to the fur as much body heat as possible. After some two weeks it will be easy to remove the hair by a simple scraping. The piece of leather becomes extremely soft, and it requires a little effort to cut large ropes or shorter leather strips*" (Gusinde, 1986 (2) I: 399).

Once dried and scraped, the leather is subjected to the process of kneading; for this the *Yamana* women use to wring and rub the leather strongly with their hands, and chew the harder parts so that the leather becomes soft with abundant saliva and chewing. "*Generally, she will chew all these pieces of leather for which she wants to achieve a particular flexibility*" (Gusinde, 1986 (2) I: 400).

The data for common use of fur conservation techniques doesn't exist, especially for these furs used for scarce clothes, because its own fat and the fat absorbed by the human body (normally, they use to impregnate them selves with fish or whale oil) was accomplishing that function (Gusinde, 1986). Nevertheless, on some occasions "one piece of leather or some particular leather object is taken and greased profoundly; even more rare was to mix fish oil with burnt clay red powder, obtaining an aglutinate mixture which was spread on the leather surface pressed by the palm of the hand. If softness and flexibility is desired for most small pieces of leather, these were impregnated by fish oil for a long time. Only frequent use will prevent leather becoming hard and stiff" (Gusinde, 1986 (2) I: 400).

THE TUNEL VII STONE TOOLS WHICH HAVE TAKEN PART IN FUR PROCESSING

By the macro and microanalysis of the Tunel VII lithic remains, the traces of use attributable to different productive activities related to leatherwork were identified (Clemente, 1996, 1997). On the surfaces of these tools were registered longitudinal cutting (27) and transversal scraping (14) actions. Also, the work on the fur in its fresh and dry state, as well as the use of abrasive elements for the treatment of this material was documented.

The tools used for cutting served principally on fresh fur. The majority (17) were used with natural edges (without any retouching), using as a support the flakes with sharp and straight edges (Fig. 1: 2). Nevertheless, ten shaped tools that show a rounding accentuated by a longitudinal action of cutting were registered (Fig. 1: 1, 3, 4 and 5). Judging by the traces of use we believe that these tools were probably used for skinning certain animals, that way the retouched side was in contact with the skin and the other, natural side, with the animal's flesh or fat (in the latter case the finely polished face penetrated more). Skinning an animal by shaped tools allowed certain advantages, and avoided damages produced by wrong moves during the work, due to better control of cutting. These tools were probably used for skinning sensitive furs skinning (such as penguins or cormorant), as well as to separate the skin of the seal with a minimum of subcutaneous fat. We don't believe that these instruments were used to skin guanacos, for several reasons: first, because its more comfortable to stretch the fur helped by blows with the fist on the inside zone, the same as Pathagonian people do with guanacos and sheep at the present (M.E. Mansur, personal communication); and second, as shows archaeological records show (only some parts of the skeleton were registered: Estévez and Vila, 1996) the guanacos were skinned and cut up at the same place of capture, as opposed to seal which were transported by canoe to the beach to be quartered there (Gusinde, 1986). If we consider the written sources on the *Yamana* as undoubtedly certain, these tools would have been used by some man to remove the furs before the quartering of the animal.

Apart from the utilities, which, as we have seen could cut fur, in the Tunel VII a series of tools (14) which were used for scraping the fur is documented. According to the results of the analysis carried out, *Yamana* use to work both on fresh (9) and dry furs (5). Morphologically only four or five tools could be denominated end-scrapers, and all the rest are instruments shaped by retouch, which is common to scrapers (Laplace, 1974; Vila, 1987).

The work on fresh furs is documented in the ethno historical record as an activity of cleaning and extraction of fat, before the fur drying. In the archaeological record of Tunel VII, this activity is reflected by the blades of nine instruments. The majority of them (7) are shaped instruments – 1 scraper and 6 scrapers -ouch, which form a steep angle (more than 45°) (Fig. 2: 1-6). On one of the scrapers used for this kind of activity (Fig. 2: 2), sheets of a yellowish residue left in a 2mm wide band are documented on its ventral face of the right blade. On the metalographic microscope, these sheets reminds one of the subcutaneous fat observed by our experimentation on instruments used to scrape fresh fur of sea lions (these adherences remain on the lithic surfaces even several years after use).

Two tools classified in this group, one scraper and one retouched fragment, show traces of use common to scraping furs with abrasives (Fig. 2: 5). According to these traces, we consider that the worked matter was fresh fur. Nevertheless, this doesn't mean that besides abrasives they didn't employed also some type of lubricant (fat, fish oil), as it was documented in the ethno historical written sources, and it was used on dry fur. This process could have been for softening the fur, which was chosen for some piece of clothing manufacture (cloak or under wears for example).

On two other instruments on the non-shaped support, which are very similar one to another, on one of its vertexes, traces of using a transversal action on fur are shown (Fig. 2:3). Both instruments belong to the same

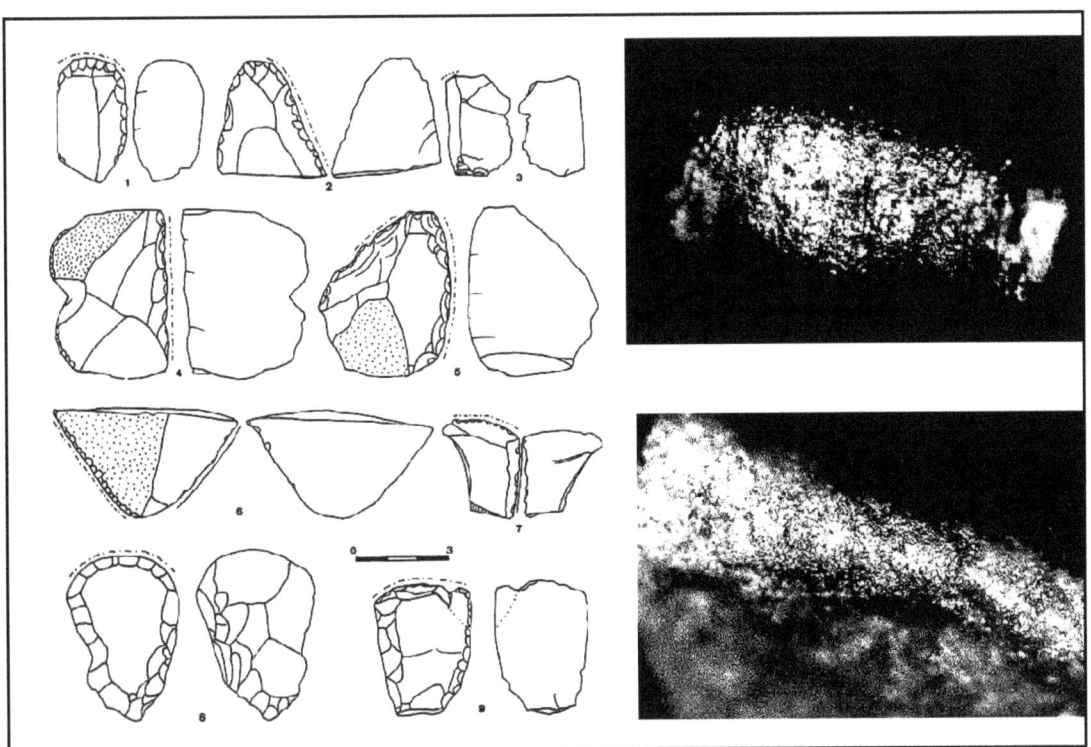

Figure 2. The Tunel VII tools used for scraping the fur/leather (left) and micropolishes by this activity -200X- (right).

ETHNO HISTORICAL SOURCES	ARCHAEOLOGICAL SOURCES
1- FUR EXTRACTION 2- CLEANING BY SCRAPING 3 -DRYING 4- DEPILATION 5- LEATHER SLIMMING 　(with, or without abrasive agents) 6- SOFTENING BY KNEADING	1- FUR EXTRACTION 　(and/or cutting of the skin) 2- CLEANING BY SCRAPING 3- DRYING 4- LEATHER SLIMMING 　(with, or without abrasive agents)

Figure 3. The activities documented by ethno historical and archaeological sources.

excavation unit (B 225 of net II). We don't have any specific explanation of the type of work in which these instruments were used, although it is possible that it was delicate work with furs (such as producing leather strips and ropes?).

All tools, which were applied in the fresh fur (or lubricated fur) processing, were used for a scraping action. Only one tool (Fig. 2: 6) shows two active edges – one retouched for scraping, and another without shaping, which was used for cutting the same material. Only on the scraper (Fig. 2: 1) we have observed on the dorsal edges various spots of shiny polish, which could be related to some kind of handle. On other instruments, as represented by n°4 en Fig. 2, the lateral opposite to the used one is blunted by an abrupt retouch, probably to avoid injuring the hand.

Five tools used for the **processing of dry fur** also show a scraping action in order to make leather thin, taking one layer of the interior side of the fur. Four of these instruments are scrapers (Fig. 2: 8-9), which probably were handled to obtain the highest efficiency. The fifth tool (Fig. 2: 7) is a fragment used without shaping: the distal edge in a scraping action and the right cutting edge for cutting the same material. According to the ethno historical sources, these activities of scraping and cutting would have been done by women.

DISCUSSION

As we have been able to confirm, the Tunel VII stone tools used in the fur processing reflects various activities. These activities are related to different phases or moments of the production process. Thus, for example, instruments used to skin an animal, others applied equally for skinning and for cutting the fur, and others used for scraping the furs have been documented. This activity is documented both, for fresh fur, to execute the first cleaning of the interior side, as well as for dry fur, to make it thin. Also, some type of abrasive in the treatment of the fur (fresh or lubricated by fat) is documented in the traces. All these activities reflected in the traces are documented in the ethno historical written sources. Nevertheless, the activity of depilation of furs wasn't registered, even knowing that it was a common practice, probably because of the specific putrefaction system used; the softening of leather by kneading, an activity executed by hands and teeth, thus leaving no traces on any instrument, wasn't registered either (Fig. N° 3).

The work on preparation of furs by transversal actions is not well represented in the lithic material of Tunel VII. It is possible to propose the hypothesis that at least some parts of this work was not carried out in the excavated zone. Another alternative or complementary hypothesis is that instruments of perishable material, which are not conserved in the archaeological record, had been used to carry out this activity. The experimentation with shell knives and functional analysis of ethnographic examples have led to the identification of functional traces, which can be related to this activity (Mansur, 1986). According to written sources (Oquera and Piana, 1999), this type of tool was widely applied to an endless number of activities. In Tunel VII some fragments of shell knives are documented, but unfortunately in very bad condition for microscopic analysis.

Author's address

Ignacio CLEMENTE CONTE
Laboratorio de Arqueología
Institución Milá y Fontanals – CSIC
C/ Egipciaques 15
08001- Barcelona (España)
mail: ignacio@bicat.csic.es

Bibliography

BRIDGES, THOMAS, 1933, *Yamana-English dictionary*. Manuscript finished cca. 1879, published by F. Hestermann and M. Gusinde with restricted cyrculation, Mödling 1933. Second publication: Natalie P. De Goodall, Zagier y Urruti Publicaciones, Ushuaia, 1987, 665 pp.

CLEMENTE CONTE, I., 1996, *Instrumentos de trabajo líticos de los yámanas (canoeros-nómadas de la Tierra del Fuego): una perspectiva desde el análisis funcional*. PhD Thesis (1995). Edició microfotográfica. Publicacions de la Universitat Autónoma de Barcelona.

CLEMENTE CONTE, I., 1997, *Los instrumentos líticos de Túnel VII: una aproximación etnoarqueológica*. Treballs d'Etnoarqueologia, 2. CSIC, UAB. Madrid.

COON, C.S., 1977, *The hunting peoples*. Pelica Books, Middlesex.

COOPER, J. 1946, The Yaghan. In: *Handbook of South American Indians*, I: 81-106.

DESPARD, G. PACKENHAM, 1859, VP Letters and fragments of his diary published in *The Voice of Pity for South America* IV a VIII (1857 a 1861). London.

ESTÉVEZ, J. & VILA, A., 1996, *Encuentros en los conchales fueguinos*. Treballs d'Etnoarqeuologia 1, UAB, CSIC.

GUSINDE, M., 1986, *Los indios de Tierra del Fuego. Los Yamana*. Tom II, three volums. Centro Argentino de Etnología Americana. CONICET, Buenos Aires.

HYADES, P.D. & DENIKER, J., 1891, Mission Scientifique du Cap Horn 1882-1883. *Anthropologie et Ethnographie*, VII, Ed. Oficial, París.

LAPLACE, G., 1974, La typologie analytique et structurale; base rationnelle d'étude des industries lithiques et osseuse. In: *Banques de dones archéologiques*. Paris: 91-143.

MANSUR-FRANCHOMME, M.E., 1984, *Préhistoire de Patagonie. L'industrie "Nivel 11" de la province Santa Cruz (Argentine): Technologie lithique et traces d'utilisation.* BAR International Series 216.

MANSUR-FRANCHOMME, M.E., 1986, *Microscopie du materiel lithique: traces d'utilisation, altérations naturelles, accidentelles et technologiques*. Cahiers du Quaternaire, n° 9, Centre National de la Recherche Scientifique, Bordeaux.

OQUERA, L.A. & PIANA, L.E., 1999, *La vida material y social de los Yámana*. Instituto Fueguino de Investigaciones Científicas. Eudeba, Universidad de Buenos Aires.

VILA, A., 1987, *Introducció a l'estudi de les eines ítiques prehistòriques*. Universitat Autónoma de Barcelona; CSIC.

INFERENCES AND LIMITATIONS IN CHIPPED-STONE MODELING: LEARNING FROM AN ETHNOARCHAEOLOGICAL CASE (THRESHING-SLEDGE PRODUCTION IN THESSALY, GREECE)

Lia KARIMALI

Abstract: Threshing-sledges are among the few well-documented stone artifacts of the ethnoarchaeological record in the Mediterranean region. The current presentation concerns the collection of data from the agricultural region of Thessaly, central Greece. As use of threshing-sledges had already ceased in the region by the early sixties, the principal aim of this research was to reconstruct the behavioral sequence and practices related to the production and distribution of the agricultural artifact (i.e., division of labor, mobility patterns etc.). The ultimate goal was to construct a comparative frame of reference (on the basis of similarity or difference) that would stimulate and expand the inferential basis in chipped-stone modeling.

As research showed, agricultural poverty was the key-factor behind any decision towards specialized production. Generally, there was never a single production system operating in the whole region of Thessaly. Different but overlapping distribution networks dominated different parts of the region depending on proximity or cultural affiliations. All these factors resulted to a largely discontinuous and complex system of overlapping networks subjected to transformations and rapid changes.

Research results are assessed in the light of their use in modeling the production of flaked prehistoric artifacts and their utility in building an inferential body of reference. As certain behavioral patterns of the ethnographic record are not directly applicable to past cultural systems, the limitations of the ethnographic research are further discussed.

Résumé : Les tribulums occupent une place importante dans la recherche ethnoarhéologique de la région méditérannéenne, étant des objets lithiques assez bien documentés. Cette présentation porte sur la production des tribulums provenant de Thessalie, une région agricole de la Grèce centrale. Lorsque l'utilisation de ces outils est arretée dans la région pendant les années '60, notre recherche a tenté de reconstituer et comprendre le comportement et la sequence des pratiques liées à la production et la distribution de cet outil agricole. Notre but majeur était de construire ainsi une base de référence comparative qui pourrait stimuler et élargir la base théorique sur laquelle s'appuient les modèles qui tentent d'expliquer la production et la distribution de l'industrie lithique taillée.

La recherche a montré que le paramètre qui imposait une production spécialisée des tribulums était la pauvreté agricole. En grandes lignes, il n'y avait jamais un seul système de production operé dans toute la région ; il s'agit plutôt de différents réseaux de distribution qui parfois se recouvrent et dominent les différentes parties de la région dépendant de la proximité ou de relations culturelles entre elles. Tous ces paramètres ont formé un système de réseaux discontinu et complex subordonné à des changements et des transformations rapides.

Les résultats de notre recherche ont été utilisés pour aborder les problèmes posés dans la production de l'industrie lithique taillée préhistorique et pour élucider le fondememt théorique des interprétations proposées. Lorsque certains aspects de l'analyse ethnographique ne peuvent pas être directememt appliqués aux systèmes culturels du passé, les limites d'une telle approche ont été prises en compte et ont été rediscutées.

THE ROLE OF ETHNOGRAPHY IN MODELING LITHIC DISTRIBUTION: GOALS AND DRAWBACKS

Traditionally, modeling of prehistoric behavior has been based on inferential reasoning. The need for constructing an inferential framework for interpreting the archaeological record was a well-taken point within the field of New Archaeology. In the 1980s, Binford (1981;1983;1987) called for the development of middle-level inferential ('warranting') arguments. Such arguments, defined as 'generalizations that attempt to account for regularities that occur between two or more sets of variables in multiple instances' (Trigger 1989:21) are based on observations in the living world. This led to the growth of ethno-archaeology (i.e.,'living archaeology','on-site' and 'off-site' informants; Gould 1977), that came to play a primary role in the interpretive process. On the basis of ethnographic analogies drawn from similar socio-economic contexts of the real world, archaeologists hoped to bridge the gap between interpretation and the static archaeological record. Yet, during the years, an ongoing debate developed on the nature and the validity of those analogies (Gifford-Gonzalez 1991, Gallay 1989, Brumbach and Jarvenpa 1990). Today, given the 'post-processual' focus on the role of perception in the interpretive process, ethno-archaeological reasoning is questioned more than ever. Although at the lower, more practical levels of analysis the construction of analogies is still pursuable (i.e., tool use identification), problems arise as ones relies on inferences at the higher, more theoretical level (i.e., parameters affecting behavior).

The mode by which systems of lithic production and distribution were organized in the past is one example of the type of questions asked at a higher level of analysis. Following the successful chemical identification of the source of obsidian in the Aegean (Melos; Renfrew et al 1965), modeling in this region has been focused on disentangling the modes of obsidian production and circulation (Runnels 1985, Torrence 1986, Perlès 1990, Kardulias 1992, Karabatsoli 1997, Karimali 2000 & 2002).

Traditionally, modeling has been grounded on inferences drawn from two main sources, cross-cultural ethnographic parallels and western theoretical frameworks. The serious drawbacks of these inferential bodies of reference were analytically discussed in a previous paper (Karimali 2000). In the current presentation a few of these inferences pertaining to models of obsidian production and distribution in the Aegean are juxtaposed to data collected from an ethnoarchaeological survey of a pre-industrial production system running in the region of modern Thessaly, central Greece until the middle of the century. The survey, conducted during the early 1990s (cf. Karimali 1994), was designed to understand the mechanics of the threshing-sledge production and circulation system in the region. As shown by the results, studying the organizational components of modern production systems can help us pinpoint differences as well as similarities to the prehistoric ones. Indeed, in our case, enlightenment of one of these systems stimulated a better understanding and refinement of several parameters used in models of obsidian production and circulation in the Neolithic Aegean.

THE THRESHING-SLEDGE:
USAGE AND ETHNOGRAPHIC EVIDENCE

Threshing sledges (*tribulum, dhoukani*) were specialised agricultural equipment, widely used for threshing in the Mediterranean (Turkey, Greece, Palestine, Spain, Portugal, and Cyprus) during the ancient and pre-industrial times.

The sledge (Fig. 1&2) is a wooden implement equipped with teeth from stone used to separate grain seeds from chaff during threshing. It consists of two wooden planks laid side by side and tied together, with their extreme end curving upwards. Each plank has 18-24 rows of blade/flakes made of varieties of chert, retouched along one edge and set into slots carved evenly by chisel. Threshing sledges were brought to threshing floors (called *alonia*) where they were dragged by a yoke of oxen or donkeys across the harvested grain. A person often sat upon a chair placed on the sledge and moved clockwise or counter-clockwise in order to separate the grain and cut the stalk efficiently.

Literary evidence of the origins of the threshing-sledge in the Mediterranean goes back as far as 2,200 BC (Akkadian tablet of the Diyala region, Pearlman 1984:16; Ataman 1999). Nevertheless, sledges are commonly presented as agricultural devises invented and/or established during the Roman period. The sledge continued to be a popular implement in many countries of the Mediterranean region until the 1950s and 1960s, when it was gradually replaced by modern farming machinery (tractor-powered threshers). Although used in all agricultural areas, little was known about its production and use all over the Mediterranean. So far, the only well-known studies are those of Bordaz (1969) and Ataman (1999) who recorded features of the threshing-sledge production system in Turkey, and Pearlman (1984) and Fox (1984) who recorded the same system in Cyprus. A few other studies have focused on the problem of identifying stones used in sledges in archaeological samples (i.e., Shakun 1999; cf. Whallon 1978, Kardulias and Yerkes 1996 on *use-wear analysis*). Recently, concern for interviewing the last flintknappers of Cyprus led to a new cycle of interest (Whittaker 1996 & 1999).

THE ORGANIZATION OF THRESHING SLEDGE
PRODUCTION IN THESSALY:
GOALS AND OBJECTIVES

Threshing sledges were also quite popular farming implements in Thessaly, central Greece. The region is renowned as the granary of modern Greece (Halstead 1989), thanks to its two extensive fertile plains (Larisa to the east and Karditsa to the west), covering an area of 3,200 km^2 of fertile land. Thus, although when the project started evidence of sledge production was poor-documented (Runnels 1990, personal communication), we considered the discovery and the location of ex-sledge producers in such a rich agricultural area an easy task. During the years 1992-3, several villages of the plain were visited, with the hope that they would yield the main body of information regarding the sledge production in the region (cf. Karimali 1994). It was soon realized, however, that communities specialized on sledge production were unlikely to be found on the vast plains of Thessaly. Given the predominant occupation of plain residents with farming, we soon discovered that it was highly unlikely that they would ever be interested in sledge production. Aided by informants, we were finally able to locate several producers at the highest mountainous areas of the region.

Specifically (cf. Fig. 3), we interviewed producers of the village of Anatoli, who were only temporarily involved in sledge production during the Nazi occupation, as well as producers from a specialized sledge production community (Kokkinopilos), founded on a high altitude of the Olympos mountains in the beginnings of the century. The consumer point of view was also provided through interviews with farmers of the plains (Megalo Monastiri). To our surprise, consumption sites did not always stay strictly adhered to consumption. Rather, it was customary to turn to independent domestic specialization when special conditions (i.e., risk, stress) appeared. This observation, along with the realization that long-term specialized production was triggered only by special conditions (i.e., agricultural poverty etc.) added one more goal to our inquiry, to detect the circumstances that favor either temporary or permanent specialized production. Thus, the objectives of the survey were formed as follows:

- Identification and characterization of the mode (s) of sledge production employed in the region, as well as its diachronic changes,
- Understanding of the special mechanics of sledge distribution in the region (i.e., along main trade routes, cultural ties etc.), and
- Detection of the special conditions favouring specialisation.

The ultimate goal was to juxtapose the modes and causes of production identified in the modern case to the archaeological expectations prevailing in the field of prehistoric exchange (cf. Renfrew 1975) and test their validity.

Figure 1. Threshing - sledge. Lower view.

LOCATING PRODUCTION AND CONSUMPTION SITES

Anatoli

The village of Anatoli, founded on the mountain of Ossa (eastern Thessaly), provided us with information regarding two periods:

- ***before the 1940s***. According to the recalls of consumers, the village was supplied by itinerant producers who were coming from a highly mountainous village (Katafigi) of mount Pieria (Macedonia). These were famous carpenters, mastering the technique of sledge manufacture for years, who made year-round trips away from home (~60-100 km) in order to find and use stone and wood resources. Upon their short visits to Anatoli, they manufactured sledges upon request, by using local

Figure 2. Threshing - sledge. Upper view.

wood (pine) and stone resources from the area around the village.

- **during the Nazi occupation and the Greek Civil War.** Information was gained by the two carpenters of the village, who decided to turn to sledge production when all trade routes connecting the village to the main city were disrupted and all other alternative means of getting sledge supplies were cut off. According to their testimony, they would choose one day of early summer to visit the nearest chert sources (1-2 km away). During their visit, they would collect suitable cobbles of whitish chert (*stournares*) after testing them carefully for possible flaws and carry them by donkey back to their village. Then they processed them at the carpenter's store, located at the village's central square. Knapping involved flaking with a heavy hammer and geared to the production of irregular flakes, which were subsequently hammered into the slots of the sledge. The wooden planks were manufactured of pine found in abundance at the village's immediate vicinity. Sledges were

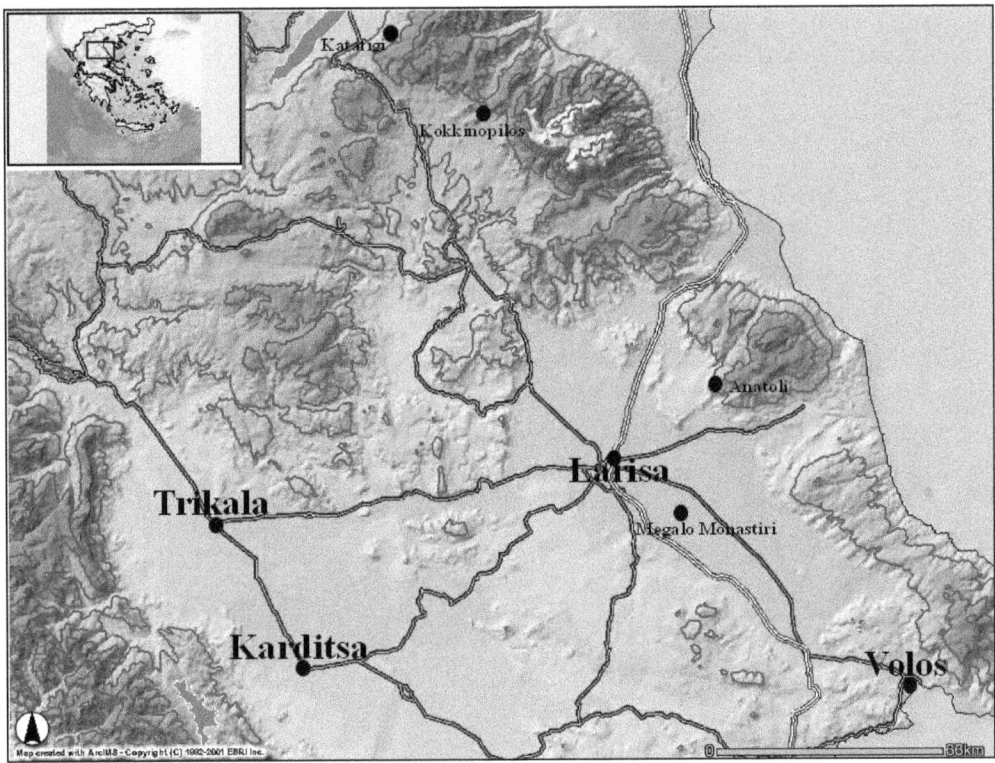

Figure 3. Map of Thessaly showing the villages discussed in the text.

exchanged for bags of wheat offered by the farmers. By the early 1950s, with the re-opening of the trade routes, the local threshing sledge production system came to an end.

In sum, the production system in Anatoli comprised two phases: one, during which the village was only a consumption unit, served by itinerant foreign producers from Katafigi, and another during which the village turned to local production. The two systems differed in terms of structure, skill and time span. The former was a formally organized production system, involving the skillful manipulation of chert and local pine by specialized producers, who by being itinerants, satisfied a wider demand in the region. In contrast, the latter was a local, rather opportunistic industry, practiced on a small scale by amateur knappers to satisfy local needs for a limited period of time. The two systems never existed side by side, rather once the former was disrupted, it was replaced by the other.

Kokkinopilos

The village of Kokkinopilos, founded on the mountain of Olympos (northern Thessaly) by Vlachs in the early century, was the second village visited during the survey. Kokkinopilos was a specialized threshing-sledge production community until the 1960s. Specialized sledge production developed on a part-time, family basis, as a safeguard mechanism against agricultural poverty. The main labor unit was confined to members of the nuclear family, namely the father, who undertook all stages of production, and his wife and children who assisted him in raw material collection and workshop maintenance.

All manufacture activities were carried out in the family's courtyard during the summer months. The family members would visit the closest sources lying at the valley of Sarantoporo to collect the most suitable cobbles for blade/flake production. Nodules of white chert (*"stournares"*) were carefully chosen after testing their quality by hammer flaking. Subsequently, they were transferred and piled up at the producer's courtyard until the wooden part of the threshing-sledge became ready (i.e., wooden planks were locally manufactured of local pine). Nodules were decorticated by men with the aid of a heavy hammer, were broken up by women into smaller blade-flakes with no special preparation and were hammered by men into the slots (Fig. 4). Slots were opened up with the aid of a steel chisel. Manufacturing waste was piled up at the peripheral zone of the courtyard until it was discarded away into river streams. Ready threshing-sledges were loaded on donkeys and distributed with direct visits to the villages of the immediate vicinity (~1 week distance, by donkeys). From the 1938 and on, sledge producers were organized to a village corporation. Distribution now was accomplished through stores located at the main big cities of Thessaly (i.e., Larisa). Unification regularized production and maximized returns. Despite its small-scale, this village industry served the farmers of the neighboring plains for almost half century until sledges came out of use.

In general, threshing-sledge production at Kokkinopilos shares similar features with the system originated from Katafigi (see above). By being highly mountainous villages, both Kokkinopilos and Katafigi had to turn to sledge production due to risky environmental conditions leading to poverty. Both villages developed specialised

Figure 4: Demonstration of flint-knapping at Kokkinopilos.

production systems, with special technical knowledge and skill transferred from generation to generation. Distribution of sledges was based on itinerant moves. Yet, there is a clear-cut difference in mobility patterns. Producers from Kokkinopilos used local stone resources available within their vicinity, produced the sledges at home, and then moved only in order to distribute them. In contrast, producers from Katafigi followed a seasonal round away from home, collecting sources around the villages they visited. The latter system (i.e., 'long-distance, year-round itinerant movement') is similar to that described in Cyprus by Pearlman (1984).

Megalo Monastiri

The village of Megalo Monastiri, inhabited by Greek-speaking immigrants from Bulgaria, is lying at the Larisa plain, 10-15 km away from the modern city of Larisa. This site provided us with a first-hand account of the consumer point of view. The village was never a production site itself, as its position on the fertile plains made farming a flourishing activity. Yet, at the same time when Anatoli was served by the itinerants from Katafigi (before the 1940s), Megalo Monastiri was supplied by fellow countrymen, that is, Bulgarian itinerant producers, who traveled long distances in order to serve its needs. Specifically, elder informants recalled a case of a Bulgarian producer who visited their village regularly in order to supply them with sledges. The latter had been manufactured in his workshop in Bulgaria. From the villagers' testimonies, it also became clear that the producer belonged to a specialized community of Bulgaria, who supplied a high number of Greek villages inhabited by Greek-speaking immigrants from the north. After the death of the producer in 1942, cultural ties with Bulgaria weakened and villagers turned to local stores and regional markets for getting their supplies.

Lastly, other informants from the same village recalled the manufacture of gunflints from stones collected from river streams, brought occasionally to the village by shepherds.

In sum, flint-knapping production activities in Megalo Monastiri had a dual character: one securing the supplies of threshing-sledges based on cultural affiliations, and on domestic, supplying gunflints (i.e., "embedded procurement").

DISCUSSION

Ethnographic fieldwork in Thessaly highlights a number of important points, outlined as follows:

1. There was never a single production system operating in the whole region of Thessaly. At the diachronic level, production networks were not static organizations conducted in the same way over the years, but active behavioral systems adjusted to the wider socio-

economic setting in which they operated. As a natural consequence, they could suddenly come into existence, subject to major structure transformations (i.e., in terms of labor structure, techniques), or cease to exist. Clearly, villages played different roles (i.e., production versus consumption) in the whole economic system, depending on the self-sufficiency of their subsistence base.

2. With regard to the prevailing modes of production and exchange, the main mode of sledge production was the specialised village industry. Such industries displayed variations in mobility, reminiscent of the types of mobility linked with hunter-gatherers (cf. 'residential and logistical mobility patterns, Binford 1980). In our case, two such variants were identified: one (Kokkinopilos) in which producers used local resources and moved at certain intervals over affordable distances only to distribute their products. Upon the delivery of their products to consumers, producers returned back to the village for new loads. And a second one (Katafigi; see also in Cyprus, Pearlman 1984), in which producers made round year trips over large distances to produce sledges upon request. Other modes of production included the village-based domestic mode and the embedded mode employed for the procurement of gunflint stones.

3. Division of labor developed mostly along family lines. At Kokkinopilos, production activities were carried out at certain parts of the residence by all family members, each having definite responsibilities. Eventually, skillful and long-lasting production established the village as expert at the market community, and thus, production became a communal activity. Unification of all family production units under the auspices of a formal corporation facilitated pursuing common goals and maximizing economic gain.

4. Distribution of merchandise followed long-term cultural ties. Due to the village, small-scale character of these industries, and the multinational features of the networks, distribution had to follow long-established cultural ties between communities sharing common ethnic-linguistic features. In other cases, proximity counted as a measure of 'relatedness' or 'familiarity' established between neighboring communities sharing common interests. This resulted to the following paradox: two neighbouring villages may not have participated in the same distribution network, as would be ideally expected. Rather, they could have been simultaneously supplied by different supplying industries linking them into separate networks, on the basis of cultural ties developed between producers and consumers. Such features underline the multi-central character of the sledge networks operating in Thessaly. Different but overlapping systems of production dominated different parts of the region, depending on several interrelated factors such as proximity, cultural affiliation, or consumption needs.

5. By all accounts, agricultural poverty was the key-factor behind any decision turning towards specialized production (cf. absence of craft- specialization in the plain). Stress conditions on the other hand, such as economic and/or cultural isolation (i.e., Nazi occupation) compelled carpenters to temporary, domestic specialization in order to insure village self-sufficiency.

ARCHAEOLOGICAL AND ETHNO-ARCHAEOLOGICAL INFERENCES: A MATTER OF ANALOGY?

Having described the organizational features of a modern production system, I return to the main question raised in the beginning of the paper: on which grounds is it legitimate to transfer cross-cultural knowledge to archaeological (lithic) modeling? For example, what is the exact relevance of the parameters brought out above to the parameters pertaining to the organization of obsidian production and distribution in the Aegean during the Neolithic? In the following paragraphs we assess the inferential basis of a few such archaeological parameters (i.e., distance, Renfrew *et al* 1965; long-distance movement of producers, Perlès 1990) in the light of the results generated from ethnoarchaeological cases and we discuss their degree of relevance.

DISTANCE. The parameter of distance plays a prominent role in any current discussion of obsidian exchange (Renfrew *et al* 1965; Torrence 1986, Perlès 1990). Fall-off models focus predominantly on distance, as being the key-variable in monitoring the quantity of material distribution in sites situated over long distances from the source. Yet, current calculations of distance in fall-off models stem from modern notions of distance, as being a stable and measurable (in km) variable. When human relations are at stake however, distance is analogous to the nexus of these relationships developed along kinship or socio-cultural ties (Karimali 2000, 2002). That was the case in our modern, pre-industrial case (Megalo Monastiri), in which products were distributed along commonly shared affiliations. Clearly, similar ties (i.e., linguistic) may not be extrapolated for the Neolithic; yet, the fact that human relationships are deeply entrenched on the degree of 'familiarity' developed among human groups assigns a new content to the concept of 'distance', with effective analogies to the Neolithic (i.e., exchange partnerships developed along kinship lines, familiarity developed on the basis of site proximity to certain loci of the landscape such as trade routes or meeting points).

LONG-DISTANCE MOVEMENT OF PRODUCERS (OR ITINERANT MODE OF PRODUCTION). It has been long accepted that members of sedentary societies are reluctant to travel long distances to obtain material goods. Due to energy and transportation costs, there is always a marginal threshold of exploitation, above which exploitation of resources is considered 'uneconomic' and is avoided (cf. Browman's 'exploitable territory thresholds model', 1976). Instead, as ethnographically demonstrated (Féblot-Augustins & Perlès 1992), materials are channeled indirectly through culturally bounded networks (cf. 'down-the-line). This results to indirect procurement systems, in which production of exchange items is likely to be discontinuous in time and space (sequential production,

Ericson 1984:4). Recently, the old preconception of the sedentary people as being attached to one place and not moving around has seriously been challenged in the light of several ethnographic testimonies (cf. Whittle's list of spectrum of movements, from residential to logistical mobility and short-term to embedded sedentism, 1997:21). Yet, these challenges do not question the long-lived ethnographic observation that sedentary consumers rarely visit distant sources (i.e., over 300 km) by themselves.

To compensate for the long-distance distribution of materials in sedentary societies, apart from the down-the-line exchange mechanism, models draw upon the mechanism of specialized traders or middlemen, for being responsible for carrying materials away from the source. The 'free-lance/middlemen' trade, or the itinerant mode of production, as a type of 'commercial trade', appears in the literature of exchange from the very beginning (cf. Renfrew's list of mechanisms of exchange, 1975). A variant of the mechanism (implying village-based rather than commercial specialization) was first employed by Perlès (1990) to account for the distribution of obsidian prepared cores to sites of the Aegean situated over 300 km away from the source of Melos. According to the model, the distribution was at the hands of specialized itinerant knappers of the continent, who prepared the cores at the source and distributed them as far as Thessaly (~300km).

Long-distance movement of itinerant producers has been ethnographically reported in various degrees (Arnold 1985; Féblot-Augustins & Perlès 1992). Yet, attention should be paid on the context in which such movement takes place. The notable difference in context for example, between the currently recorded ethnographic groups (i.e., pre-industrial societies) and the Neolithic sedentary societies should not be overlooked.

The long, round trips of knappers from northern Cyprus to the south (200 km; Pearlman 1984:124), or the Katafigi producers from Macedonia to Thessaly (max. 100 km) are cases of village-based specialization running within modern states, in the absence of territorial boundaries. In the case of Megalo Monastiri, where the thresholds of an extra-national network (Bulgarian) are attested, the partitioning of the landscape into states guarantees cross-national, long-distance movement of producers. Similarly, in the ethnographic record round-trip movement of producers is reported mainly in historical or pre-industrial cases, where modern transportation is employed. Certainly, this is true for ceramic producers: as Arnold's (1980, 1985) detailed survey of ethnographic sources pertaining to ceramic production has shown, only in cases in which modern transportation (railroad, cart or truck) is employed producers exceed the maximum distance threshold of 7-9 km for clay and temper.

Obviously, among sedentary groups non-linked by linguistic or national ties mobility contexts are expected to have counted differently. In the latter case, long distance movement would be seriously jeopardized by the multi-cultural partitioning of the landscape. Producers would be seriously dissuaded from making long-distance, round trips to obtain resources in cases 'where the source is some distance away, or the country between is peopled' (Sillitoe 1978:266). The only group widely reported to be able to penetrate distant lands is that of the middlemen, specialized in seafaring and long-distance movement (Harding 1967). For all these reasons, it is suggested that the round-based, itinerant mode of production should be applied to prehistory with caution, given the specific conditions needed to warrant safe communication.

DIVISION OF LABOR: The most notable difference between the production unit of a prehistoric and a pre-industrial, village-based industry is structure. Obviously, in the pre-industrial cases we examined, labor was evenly distributed to the members of the nuclear family or to the men of the village, when a village corporation was founded. In prehistory, the most notable residential and social unit was the extended family or the lineage, a fact pointing to a different division of labor in prehistoric settings.

CAUSES OF SPECIALIZATION: As shown by the pre-industrial cases we examined, agricultural poverty, as well as conditions of stress, were the main causes turning villagers to specialized production. That resulted to a pattern in which only villages founded on high altitudes had to turn to specialization. Yet, habitation of marginal areas in Greece dates back to the historical periods. As recent surveys of Thessaly show (Gallis 1992), in all Neolithic periods there was a clear preference for plain habitation. In contrast, human presence was minimal on the mountains. Clearly, poverty in the Neolithic owned more to risky environmental conditions (i.e., floods, extreme weather conditions; Halstead 1989) and less to settling on mountainous habitation zones.

THE CONCURRENT PRESENCE OF EXCHANGE MECHANISMS: The observation that a number of exchange mechanisms occur concurrently, linking villages to different networks is a well-taken point in recent models of obsidian distribution in the Aegean (Perlès 1990). This pattern, best exemplified by innumerable ethnographic and historical cases (cf. Féblot-Augustins & Perlès 1992), was also ascertained by our survey. Fluidity in distribution patterns is inextricably linked to fluidity in human relationships along which networks operate, and that can be considered a norm in past and present.

EPILOGUE

This paper calls for caution in using inferences drawn from modern or historical ethnoarchaeological cases to prehistory. As shown, certain behavioral patterns observed in the ethnographic record are not directly applicable to past cultural systems. Moreover, systems of production acting within different social and political/historical contexts have different aspects, and thus, they should not be analogically related. Given the important differences in context between pre-industrial and prehistoric societies, it is postulated that inferences drawn from the former to interpret the latter, should be treated with caution. After all, scrutinizing the ethnographic record is only the beginning for discovering a world of differences and varieties.

Author's address

Lia KARIMALI
Institute of Mediterranean Studies
Rethymnon, CRETE

Bibliography

ARNOLD, D.E., 1980, Localized Exchange: An Ethnoarchaeological Perspective. In *Models and Methods in Regional Exchange*, edited by R.E. Fry. SAA Papers 1, p. 147-150.

ARNOLD, D.E., 1985, *Ceramic Theory and Cultural Process*. Cambridge University Press.

ATAMAN, K., 1999, Threshing sledges and archaeology. In *Prehistory of Agriculture: New Experimental and Ethnographic Approaches*, edited by P.C Anderson. Los Angeles: University of California Press, p. 211-22.

BINFORd, L.R., 1980, Willow Smoke and Dogs' Tails: Hunter-gatherer Settlement Systems and Archaeological Site Formation. *American Antiquity* 45, 1, p. 4-20.

BINFORD, L.R., 1981, *Bones: Ancient Men and Modern Myths*. New York, Academic Press.

BINFORD, L.R., 1983, *Working at Archaeology*. New York, Academic Press.

BINFORD, L.R., 1987, Researching ambiguity: frames of reference and site structure". In *Method and Theory for Activity Area Research. An Ethnoarchaeological Approach*, edited by S. Kent, New York:Columbia University Press, p. 449-511.

BORDAZ, J., 1969, Flint Flaking in Turkey. *Natural History*, 78, p. 73-79.

BROWMAN, D., 1976, Demographic Correlations of the Wari Conquest of Junin. *American Antiquity*, 41, p. 465-477.

BRUMACH H.J., & JARVENPA R., 1990, Archaeologist-ethnographer-informant relations: The dynamics of ethnoarchaeology in the field. In *Powers of Observation: Alternative Views in Archaeology*, edited by S.M. Nelson & A. Kehoe, American Anthropological Association, p. 39-46.

ERICSON, J.E. 1984, Towards the analysis of lithic production systems. In *Prehistoric quarries and lithic production*, edited by J.E. Ericson and B.A. Purdy, Cambridge: Cambridge University Press, p. 1-9.

FÉBLOT-AUGUSTINS, J., & PERLÈS, C., 1992, Perspectives ethnoarchéologiques sur les échanges à longue distance. In *Ethnoarchéologie: Justification, Problèmes, Limites*, edited by F. Audouze, A. Gallay and V. Roux, XII Rencontres Internationales d' Archéologie et d' Histoire d' Antibes, Éditions APDCA, Juan-les-Pins, p. 195-209.

FOX, W., 1984, Dhoukani Flake Blade Production in Cyprus. *Lithic Technology* 14, p. 62-67.

GALLAY, A., 1989, Logicism: A French View of Archaeological Theory Founded in Computational Perspective. *Antiquity*, 63, p. 27-39.

GALLIS, K., 1992, *Atlas Proistorikon Oikismon tis Anatolikis Thessalikis Pediados*. Larissa.

GIFFORD-GONZALEZ, D., 1991, Bones Are Not Enough: Analogues, Knowledge and Interpretative Strategies in Zooarchaeology. *Journal of Anthropological Archaeology*, 10, p. 215-254.

GOULD, R.A., 1977, Ethno- archaeology; or where do models come from? A closer look at Australian Aboriginal lithic technology. In *Stone Tools as Cultural Markers: Change, Evolution and Complexity*, Prehistory and Material Culture Series, edited by R.V.S. Wright. Australian Institute of Aboriginal Studies, Canberra, No 12, p. 162-168.

HALSTEAD, P.L.J., 1989, The Economy has a Normal Surplus: Economic Stability and Social Change among Early Farming Communities of Thessaly, Greece. In *Bad Year Economics. Cultural Responses to Risk and Uncertainty*, edited by P. Halstead and J. O'Shea, Cambridge: Cambridge University Press, p. 68-80.

HARDING, T.G., 1967, *Voyagers of the Vitiaz Strait. A Study of a New Guinea Trade System*. Seattle and London: University of Washington Press.

HARTENBERGER, B., & RUNNELS, C., 2001, The Organization of Flaked Stone Production at Bronze Age Lerna. *Hesperia* 70, p. 255-283.

KARABATSOLI, A., 1997, *La Production de l'Industrie Lithique Taillée en Grèce Centrale pendant le Bronze Ancien*, Thèse, Université de Paris X.

KARIMALI, L., 1994, *The Neolithic Mode of Production and Exchange Reconsidered: Lithic Production and Exchange Patterns in Thessaly, Greece, during the Transitional Late Neolithic-Bronze Age Period*. A Ph.D. Dissertation, Boston University.

KARIMALI, L., 2000, Decoding inferences in models of obsidian exchange:contexts of value transformation in the Neolithic Aegean. In *Trade and Production in Premonetary Greece. Proceedings of the 6th International Workshop, Athens 1996*, edited by C.Gillis, C. Risberg and B.Sjöberg. Paul Åströms förlag, p. 9-27.

KARIMALI, L., 2002, Redifining the variables of material abundance and distance in the fall-off models: The Case of Neolithic Thessaly. In *Archaeometry Studies for Greek Prehistory and Antiquity*, edited by G. Basiakos, E. Aloupi & G. Fakorellis, Athens, p. 753-761.

KARDULIAS, P.N., 1992, The Ecology of Bronze Age Flaked Stone Tool Production in Southern Greece: Evidence from Agios Stephanos and the Southern Argolid. *American Journal of Archaeology* 96, p. 421- 442.

KARDULIAS P.N., &.YERKES R.W., 1996, Microwear and metric Analysis of Threshing Sledge Flints from Greece and Cyprus. *Journal of Anthropological Science* 23, p. 657-666.

PEARLMAN D., 1984, *Threshing Sledges in the Eastern Mediterranean:Ethnoarchaeology with Chert Knappers*, Master Thesis, University of Minnesota, Minnesota.

PERLÈS, C., 1990, L' outillage de pierre taillée Néolithique en Grèce:approvisionnement et exploitation des matières premières. *BCH 114*, p. 1-42.

RENFREW, C., 1975, Trade as action at a distance: A question of integration and communication. In *Ancient Civilization and Trade*, edited by J. A. Sabloff and C. C. Lamberg-Karlovsky, Albuquerque: University of New Mexico Press, p. 3-60.

RENFREW, C., CANN, J.R., & DIXON, J.E., 1965, Obsidian in the Aegean. *Annual of the British School at Athens*, 60, p. 225-247.

RUNNELS, C., 1985, The Bronze-Age Flaked-Stone Industries from Lerna: A Preliminary Report. *American Journal of Archaeology* 54, p. 357-391.

RUNNELS, C., 1990, personal communication.

SHAKUN, N., 1999, Evolution of agricultural techniques in Eneolithic (Chalcolithic) Bulgaria: Data from use-wear analysis. In *Prehistory of Agriculture:New Experimental and Ethnographic Approaches*, edited by P.C Anderson, Los Angeles: University of California Press, p. 199-210.

SILLITOE, P., 1978, Ceremonial exchange and trade: two contexts in which objects change hands in the Highlands of Papua New Guinea. *Mankind* 11, p. 265-75.

TORRENCE, R., 1986, *Production and Exchange of Stone Tools Prehistoric Obsidian in the Aegean*, Cambridge University Press, Cambridge.

TRIGGER, B., 1989, *A History of Archaeological Thought*, Cambridge University Press, Cambridge.

WHALLON, R., 1978, Threshing Sledge Flints: a Distinctive Pattern of Wear. *Paléorient* 4, p. 319-324.

WHITTAKER, J., 1996, Athkiakas: A Cypriot flintknapper and the threshing sledge industry. *Lithic Technology* 21, p. 108-20.

WHITTAKER, J., 1999, Alonia:The Ethnoarchaeology of Cypriot Threshing Floors. *Journal of Mediterranean Archaeology* 12.1, p. 7-25.

WHITTLE, A., 1997, Moving on and Moving around: Neolithic Settlement Mobility. In *Neolithic Landscapes*. Group Seminar Papers 2, edited by P. Topping. Oxbow Monographs 86, p. 15-22.

ANALYSIS OF AN ARCHAEOLOGICAL GRINDING TOOL: WHAT TO DO WITH ARCHAEOLOGICAL ARTEFACTS?

Débora ZURRO, Roberto RISCH & Ignacio CLEMENTE CONTE

Abstract: This paper aims to offer an alternative approach to conventional (and often even non-existent) studies of macrolithic or ground stone tools found in archaeological contexts. The analysis of a unique artefact, a "mano", from an ethnographic context (Dogon country, Mali), is used to develop a methodological model for the daily archaeological research of this type of material. From the standpoint that labour processes (which are materialised in archaeology mainly as tools and finished products) are the key elements in the understanding of prehistoric societies, we propose a methodology which integrates use-wear analysis (addressing the participation of the tool in the productive cycle) and residue analysis (allowing an understanding of the processed good). The combination of both techniques should allow us to make evident a series of materials and working processes that have hardly been documented in the archaeological record until now, or even remain unknown.

Résumé : Cet article a l'objective d'offrir une alternative aux études classiques concernant le macro-outillage provenant des contextes archéologiques. L'analyse d'un unique outil, dans ce cas une « mano » provenant d'un contexte ethnographique (pays Dogon, Mali) a été réalisé afin d'obtenir un modèle méthodologique à suivre dans notre recherche archéologique quotidienne. Partant de la prémisse que les processus de travail (lesquels sont habituellement matérialisés dans les gisements archéologiques sous forme d'instruments et de produits/biens) constituent l'aspect primordial qui va nous permettre arriver au connaissance des sociétés préhistoriques, nous considérons nécessaire la combinaison de l'analyse tracéologique (qui constate la participation de l'instrument dans le cycle productive) et l'analyse des résidus conservés sur des surfaces des outils (qui permet une approximation aux matériaux processés). La combinaison de ces deux techniques devrait nous permettre rendre en évidence dans le registre archéologique des processus de travail et des matériaux transformés qui n'ont pas été jusqu'à maintenant documentés.

INTRODUCTION

Macrolithic or ground stone tools comprise a wretched category among prehistoric artefacts. Despite their good preservation and frequency in the archaeological record, these objects are only mentioned superficially, if at all, in most excavation reports, and are seldom seen to deserve a thorough petrographic and technological study. Systematic recording carried out on some exceptional excavations (e.g. Zimmermann 1988; Risch 1995; Böhner 1997; Stranini and Voytek 1997; Castro et al. 1999) encourages the suspicion that thousands of stone tools usually end on the spoilheap or, less likely, are stored in deposits of archaeological museums[1]. This "sampling strategy" contrasts, at least in the later Prehistoric sites of the Western Mediterranean, with the exhaustive documentation and study of pottery, bone, metal, wooden or flaked stone tools, materials which tend to appear in small quantities or are more likely to be affected by taphonomic processes (fragmentation, degradation, etc.), which limit their heuristic potential.

The marginal attention paid to macrolithic artefacts is also surprising in view of their importance as the technical means of many production processes in prehistoric, but also historical times. Grinding, pounding, polishing, burnishing, hammering, cutting or casting are some of the activities which can be carried out with stone tools. Therefore, societies have developed a great variety of tool types which were used to process grain and other plants, meat or skin, in pottery production, metal working, mining, etc. Many activities can only be identified in the archaeological record by means of the stone artefacts employed. Given that the final products obtained are destined to and transformed in the consumption process, these tools are also an important means for quantifying the volume of production. Consequently, it must be argued, that any archaeological approach concerned with questions like "what", "how" and "how much" was produced by a society, implies a definition of the technical means of production, where stone artefacts have played a significant role until historic times.

The claim for a more rigorous analysis of the ground stone assemblages has been made repeatedly in the last decades (e.g. Kraybill 1977; Wright 1992). Yet, although some methodological and empirical progress has been achieved, it still holds true that, in general, these archaeological materials are analysed and published in an insufficient way. Thus, aspects which are crucial in order to understand the development of the forces of production in different societies, such as the morpho-technological changes of tools and their spatial distribution during later Prehistory, remain unknown.

The reasons for such research deficiencies seem to be diverse: the weight of the stone assemblages causes transport and storage difficulties; many artefact types are considered uninteresting because of their rough aspect and, in Binford's terms, "expedient" character; for similar reasons they can hardly be used in chrono-typological studies, which still play an important role in European

---

[1] Just to give an approximate figure of the volume of stone tools which can be expected in prehistoric settlements of the western Mediterranean: in a systematically excavated multi-phase Bronze Age site like Gatas (Almería), were all sediment is sieved, 345 tools were recovered in only 60 m².

Figure 1.

archaeology; their geological, morphometrical and functional variability requires a combination of different analytical approaches (geology, petrography, material behaviour, typology, functional analysis). Yet, in our view, the main difficulty lies in the insufficient development of a research methodology, which allows the understanding and explanation of these artifacts in relation to the productive processes and economic structures of which they formed part. Interpretative models are necessary that give meaning to the natural resources used, the observed morphometrical variables and the use-wear patterns (e.g. Hayden 1979, 1987; Adams 1989, 1993; Risch 1995, 2002).

One way to progress in our understanding of the natural, formal and technical parameters involved in the formation of a stone tool is through analysis of social and economic contexts where these materials are still used (e.g. Horsfall 1987; Baune 1989; Gronenborn 1994). Such approaches allow the testing and improvement of the methodology of ground stone studies, and the gathering of reference patterns for our archaeological observations. The present study applies a series of functional analyses of a grinding instrument collected by one of us in 2000 at the Bandiagara fault in Southeast Mali. This artefact was being used by Dogon women in order to produce millet flour in grinding areas placed on a large medium and coarse grained sedimentary rock (Fig. 1).

A quartzite river cobble was used as a grinding tool, which, apparently, required no specific shaping process. Nearly all sides the natural surface were altered through working processes. Macroscopically, polished surfaces are visible on the obverse and reverse sides, while the top, left and right sides present a rough aspect (Fig. 2). The length, width and thickness of the tool are 10, 9, and 3.9 cm respectively. Compared with the type of tool recorded in American Indian contexts, these dimensions are rather small for a "mano" which was used with two hands during the grinding process.

In the numerous settlements of the Dogon country, which are distributed on the high plateau, as well as at the foot of the Bandiagara fault and in the plain which extends from here to Burkina Faso, one observes the use of different wooden mortars and grinding stones for the production flour (especially millet) and/or oils (peanut). The economy of these villages is based on agriculture and some husbandry. Millet is the main crop and plots of rice, onions and other agricultural products exist in the area of the fault, where small dams for irrigation have been build. The Dogon take great care in the construction of granaries in which grain and flour are stored. They are build on platforms, that isolate the products from the rain, roofed with straw and they present only a small opening, such as a window or door, which allows access to the stored products. Each family owns several of these constructions and female granaries can by distinguished from male buildings. While the first present four compartments in which different types of grain and spices are stored, the male granaries only store millet ears in a single room. The

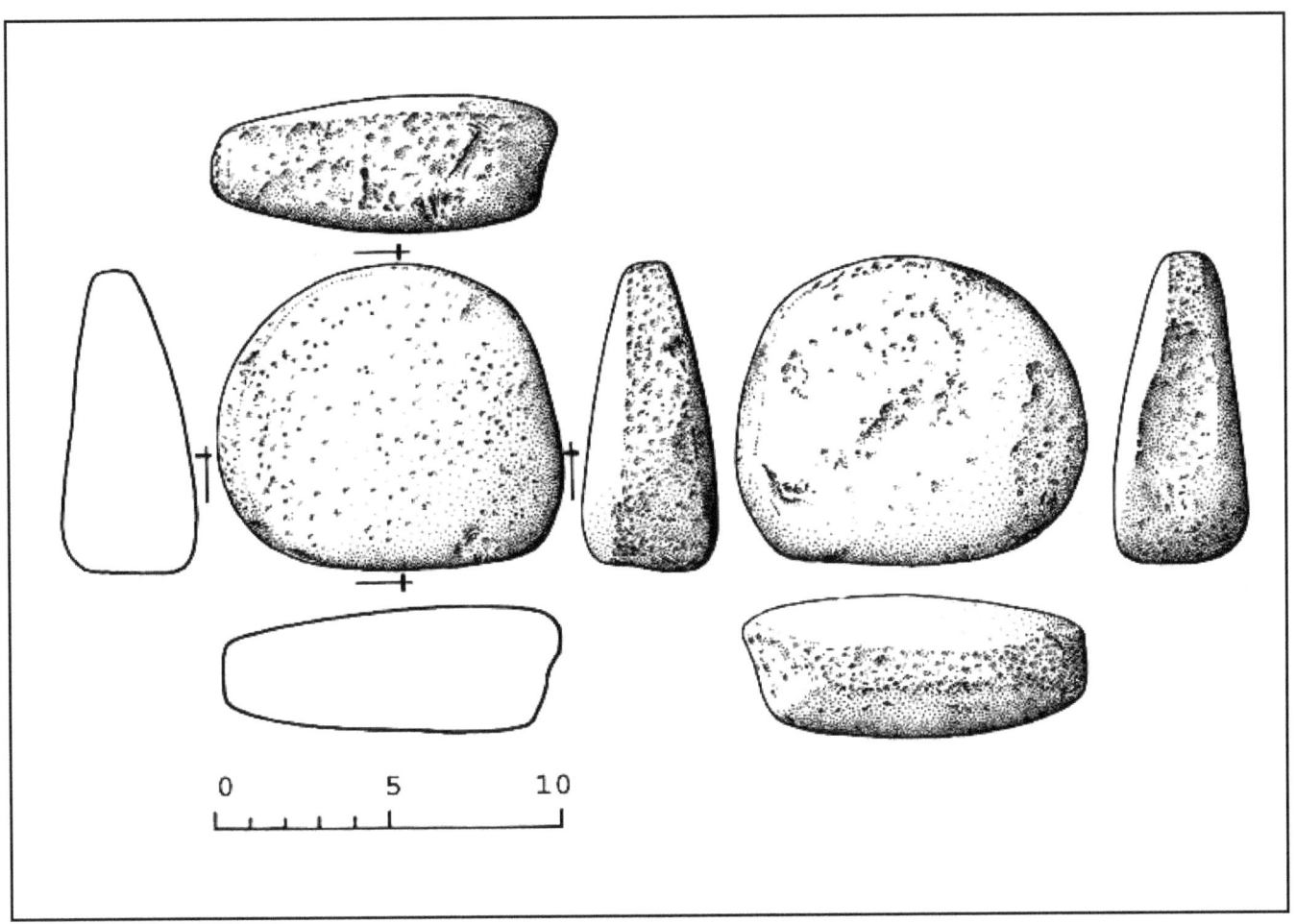

Figure 2.

wife provides the family with food over the whole year, and when her stock is exhausted, the husband continues grain distribution, underlining in this way his control over the basic subsistence product.

Apart from movable querns in domestic contexts, grinding areas also exist outside the villages. The area to which the "mano" studied belongs is located immediately above the Bandiagara fault, next to millet fields, and the distance to the nearest two villages is approximately 1 km. The "grinding platform" presented 4 grinding basins, and around them a series of "manos" were placed. In total 6 handstones could be recorded, but their association with the basins presented an irregular pattern (3, 2, 1 and 0 "manos" x basin). This millet processing complex was not used on a daily basis, but only occasionally, apparently when other activities where carried out in the area.

In order to analyse the plentiful residues present on the active surfaces of the collected "mano" a simple brushing was enough to obtain a minimal sample necessary for microscopic observation. In order to document the use-wear all residues had to be removed from the tool. Therefore the stone was subjected to an ultrasonic bath for 20 minutes, but numerous starch grains remained attached to the surface. A new bath took place, using this time a 10% HCl to allow an easier cleaning of the pores. A thin covering of white and black particles was still present at some points, showing the resilience of this type of residue (Fig. 3).

MESOSCOPIC FUNCTIONAL ANALYSIS

Semenov (1981) already considered the study of macrolithic tools, such as axes, mortars, polishers or so called arrow straighteners, when he introduced use-wear analysis to archaeology. Contrary to what has occurred since then with chipped stone industries, the development of functional analysis related to other stone artefacts is limited (see, mainly, Hayden 1979, 1987; Adams 1989, 1993; Risch 1995, 2002).

Semenov, as well as more recent studies, have applied a mesoscopic approach, analysing this type of artefact under 10-80X. One reason is that the field of observation is frequently more important than magnification in order to identify the type of alteration produced on the granular rock surfaces. Still, the potential of high power or ESM observations is a field which should be tested in the future (see below).

Based on our own experiences with functional analysis of experimental and archaeological tools, the following use-wear traits are considered relevant in a mesoscopic approach:

Figure 3.

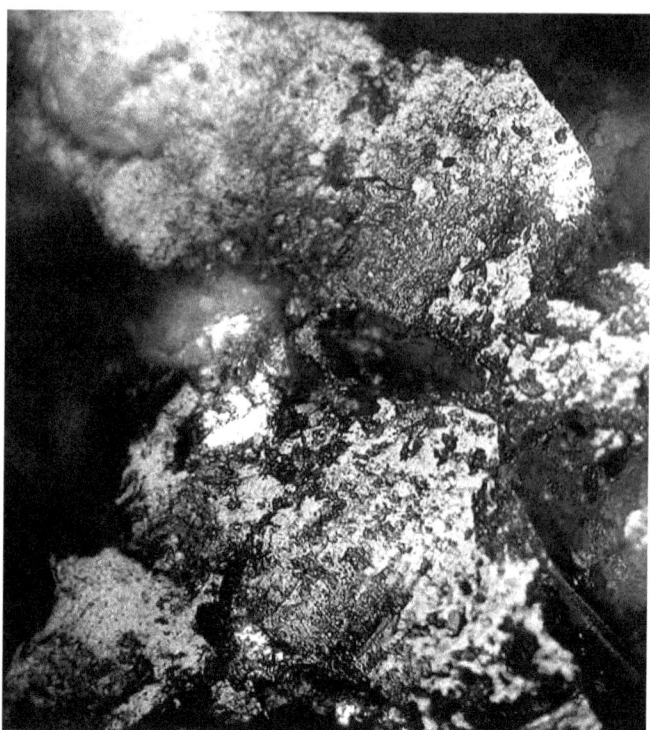

Figure 4.

Figure 4.

1. linear traces (Semenov 1981), were striations (width < 0.5 mm) or scratches are differentiated (width >0.5 mm);

2. polish or sheen (Semenov 1981);

3. plaque (Hayden 1987: 87-88);

4. edge-rounding (Hayden 1979: 18-19; Adams 1989);

5. leveling (Adams 1989);

6. grain aggregate or extraction (Hayden 1987: 86; Adams 1993);

7. frosted appearance (Hayden 1979; Adams 1989);

8. pitting (Hayden 1987: 86-87; Adams 1989; 1993);

9. checks (Hayden 1987: 85-86);

10. fractures, which can classified into concoidal or stepped fractures (Hayden 1979: 19, 1987: 91);

11. crushing or shattering (Sussman 1988: 17; Hayden 1979: 19, 1987: 89-91).

An important aspect among abrasive artefacts is the description of the topography of the surfaces and the degree of invasiveness of the use-wear (Adams 1993). In qualitative terms, it is therefore useful to differentiate during microscopic observation between a high, middle and low microtopography.

One of the main factors that affects the appearance of wear traces is the mineralogical composition, grain size and grain organization (fabric) of the rock used as a tool. The same activity can produce different types of use patterns depending on the type of raw material. Therefore, it is important to undertake a detailed petrographic description and to describe the wear traces visible on each mineral/grain type present in the artefact.

The artefact collected at the Bandiagara fault is a fine-grained (c. 0.1-0.3 mm) quartzite cobble stone, with a very homogeneous grain structure. Previous analysis of experimental tools has shown that quartz and quartzite tools develop different abrasive wear traces, than basalt, diabase or gabbro. While under macro- and mesoscopic observation striations are a characteristic feature of the later, they appear less developed on quartz (Broadent 1979; Risch 1995).

Practically all sides of the clast present alterations of the natural surface. Only the bottom part does not seem to have been used actively (fig. 1). While a smooth surface can be observed on the obverse and reverse sides, the top, left and right faces present a rough aspect (Fig. 2, 3 and 4).

Obverse and reverse side

The dominant feature under mesoscopic observation (45X) is an intense leveling of the quartz grain (Fig. 3). Yet, the surfaces are not completely smooth or flat, but show a slight asperity. This factor appears to limit the development of polish or sheen. The margins of the grain can present microfractures. The shallow interstices between the quartz grains seem to be slightly worn out, indicating adhesive wear (Adams 1993). Another important wear trace is grain extraction. No use-wear traits extend into the resulting pits, i.e. into a low topography. Fine, more or less parallel striations are hardly visible, while scratches occur occasionally.

These use-wear traits correspond to a large degree with the observations made on experimental and archaeological grain processing artefacts, made out of sandstone, vesicular basalt and psamitic shists. The patterns usually reported for stone against stone contact with vegetal intermediate material are leveling of the grain surfaces, fractures of the grain edges, pits caused removal of grains or grain aggregates, scratches and striations on the high topography, and superficial sheen, in case oily substances are ground. The leveled surfaces do not present a completely smooth aspect, as is the case, for example, after a stone against wood contact (Adams 1989, 1993; Risch 1995, 2002).

It is interesting to point out that the active surfaces of the artefact extend slightly from the obverse and reverse sides to the bottom part. Moreover, the active surface on both sides are divided into an upper and lower facet, separated through a slight ridge where abrasion is less intense. These features are the result of the way in which the artefact was operated during the grinding process, and confirm the model proposed by Adams (1999: 482; fig. 4), based on experimental grain processing tools. Two faceted use-surfaces on "manos" are indicative of working in basin (concave) grinding stones with a reciprocal, rocking stroke, which actually is the grinding technique observed in Southeast Mali. Here the pressure produced with the away-stroke is prolonged by slightly elevating the front part of the "mano", which allows the active use of the margins of the bottom side of the artefact, and produces the described downward enlargement of the lower use-facet.

The only differences between the obverse and reverse active surfaces are the intensity of the abrasive traces, and the adhered residues. Use-wear on the first presents a more developed or "fresher" appearance, and its surface was covered, before cleaning, with the white flour adherences described. The reverse side presents mainly dark residues, which are also very extended on the top, left and right sides. The aspect of both the white and black particles is practically the same, and despite the intense cleaning process, part of these residues continued to appear adhered as a film in the interstices of the stone surface (Fig.3). In both cases we seem to be dealing with flour remains, which were pressed onto the surface during the intense grinding process. The colour differences must be caused by a chemical alteration of the residues after some time of exposure of the tool in the open air. After each working session the quartzite "manos" were left on the bedrock, next to the grinding basins. While the white adherences had formed during the activities that had just taken place when the "mano" was collected, the black coloured residues correspond to a previous session. Unfortunately the periodicity of these grain processing activities at the Bandiagara fault could not be confirmed, although a yearly cycle is probable.

It is interesting to point out that this type of thin adherence of black residues has also been observed occasionally in grain interstices on the surfaces of prehistoric grinding stones from Southeast Spain, which clearly were used for grain processing. Closer analyses have not been carried out so far. The high resistance of these remains to degradation processes might imply that here we have a further functional indicator for this type of activities.

Top, left and right sides

All three sides show a continuous irregular, pitted surface (Fig. 4). Such intense material extraction is caused by impact loosening or pulverising of the grains. A second use-wear trait is the edge-rounding, produced by an abrasive processes which eliminates the sharp edges of the quartz grains at a high topography. Grains at a lower topography maintain their natural edges, indicating that the use-wear is not penetrating in the interstices, i.e. that we are dealing with percussive activities on hard materials, such as rocks. Large concoidal fractures occur very occasionally at the margins of the pitted surfaces, invading the obverse and reverse sides (fig. 1). Given the hardness of quartzite and according to experimental models of use-wear development, all these features are considered to be characteristic of intense and/or prolonged percussion on stone surfaces (Risch 2002: 128-131).

Such use-wear patterns also closely resemble the blunted prehistoric celts from Guatemala described by Hayden (1987: 96-101), and which are still (re)used today for repecking grinding stones. Here the raw materials are mainly greenstones with a grain size ranging between 0.01-0.5 mm. The most distinctive use-wear observed on the blunted celt edges is an irregular topography, caused mainly by pronounced pitting. Also in this case macro-fractures can occur in limited numbers (0-4) at the margins of the edges. Rounding of the grains is not reported in this case, possibly due to the low magnification used (generally 12X), but abrasive wear is visible on the microphotographs (Hayden 1987: 98).

All these pitted surfaces have a dark colour, produced by the presence of the same type of residues adhered in the grain interstices, as observed on the reverse side of the artefact (Fig. 4). Two conclusions can be drawn from these occurrences. First, the top, left and right sides also interacted with the processed cereal grain or flour. Second, these active surfaces were used, as the reverse side, in a previous working session and not recently, given the absence of white particles. In conclusion, it seems that this artefact had been used for working by percussion of a stone surface covered with flour. As we have no indication at the site that millet was processed through pounding, and given that such an activity is not expected to cause the observed use-wear patterns, the lateral sides of the stone tool must have served for re-roughening the grinding basins, when these became flat and their efficiency

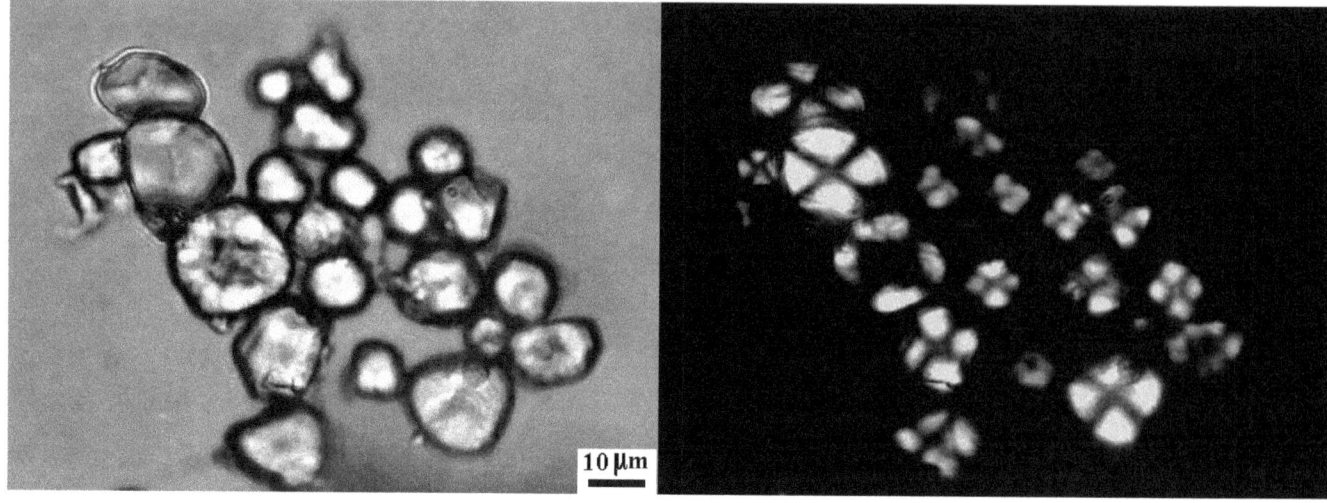

Figure 5.   Figure 6.

declined. The fact that millet flour covers the whole activity area at Bandiagara and is not removed systematically (Fig. 1), explains the presence of flour adherences on the pecking surfaces. Re-sharpening is an occasional activity[2], and was probably not carried out in all grinding basins during each grinding session.

MICROSCOPIC FUNCTIONAL ANALYSIS

Microscopic use-wear traces are visible on the obverse and reverse sides of the artefact, although they appear more developed on one of them. The traces are distributed significantly over those areas which have received more contact and pressure with the grinding basin. At a macroscopic level, such surfaces present a specific sheen and allow the reconstruction of the cinematic of the instrument. Through a metallographic microscope one observes a micropolish with a compact development on the highest topography, which is bright and not massive and whose aspect is between smooth and rough[3] (Fig. 5). In general, this type of micropolish brings to mind experimentally produced traces through contact between two lithic materials (friction of stone against stone). Nevertheless, it seems to have more volume and a smoother aspect, possibly due to the contact with the processed grain.

RESIDUE ANALYSIS

Most perishable products, and particularly materials of vegetable origin, only appear occasionally, under exceptional conditions of preservation in archaeological sites or as vegetable residues such as phytoliths, silica skeletons or starch grains. These residues present a high durability and resistance to dissolution, as well as to percolation (Therin 1994).

Starch, as a reserve substance, is especially localised in certain parts of the plant (seeds, tubers, roots and fruits) and forms the basic component of vegetable flours. Therefore, it is especially important in the study of grinding stones, as it allows the confirmation of their function in ambiguous cases as well as a more specific determination of the processed species.

The analysis of starches began in the 19th century (Nägeli, Mayer), but it was not adopted as an archaeological technique until recently (Loy 1994, Piperno et al. 2000, Therin et al. 1999), being applied primarily in certain geographical areas (Mesoamerica and Australia).

In the case of the stone tool from Mali, after the extraction of the residues, these were washed in a centrifuge with distilled water at 2,000 r.p.m. for 3 minutes (three consecutive times). Finally they were disposed, in parallel, on slides with distilled water and with a synthetic resin (Eukitt) for observation under the microscope (Olympus BX-51 at 400x).

The identification of starch grains can be carried out with different methods (Loy 1994), although the most common and straightforward one is the verification of the presence of the extinction cross or *hilum*, which can be seen with the optical microscope under polarised light. The *hilum* results out from the molecular structure of the grains (Esau 1969) and produces birrefrigence and optical anisotropy. Its morphological variation can be used as a key to plant identification, by comparing archaeological samples with known present day materials from the reference collection. Usually employed **variables** are the form and composition of the grain (simple or composed), as well as the form of the extinction cross (Loy 1994). At its present stage of development, this research method does not allow us to achieve a very precise identification of the taxa. Apart

---

[2] Depending on factors such as rock type, use intensity, or tool shape, resharpening frequencies can range from once every five days to once every year (Horsfall 1987: 341). The average repecking interval reported for metates from Mesoamerica made of vesicular basalt is 3 months (s.d. = 1.8) (Hayden 1987: 96).

[3] The description of the micropolish follows the definitions proposed by González e Ibáñez (1994) and Clemente (1997).

from pioneering works (unfortunately rare and not reprinted), carried out in the middle of the 19th century, we have a preliminary and partial classification elaborated by Czaja (1978) which allows a distinction between different families.

In this case, as the tool comes from an ethnographic context and it was known to us that the processed species was common millet (Panicum milliaceum L.), the residue analysis was carried out in order to test the method and to verify the processed material. First, some common millet grains (approximately 20-30 grammes) were powdered with a domestic coffee mill, sieving the resulting flour with a 0.100 mm sieve. The residue obtained was stored and slides for microscopy were prepared with distilled water and, again, with Eukitt. At the same time, a small reference collection was achieved with some of the species that are cultivated in Mali (Sorghum, Oryza sativa L. and Zea mays). Morphological features (polyhedric and simple grains with a central hilum) and size coincide clearly with common millet (Fig. 6), while corn presents certain similarities and rice or sorghum are absolutely dissimilar. This result confirms the potential of residue analysis in the identification of the species processed with stone tools, when a good reference collection is available.

CONCLUSIONS

The aim of the present study was to show the potential of ground stone tool analysis, and to present some reference patterns for the functional analysis of archaeological artefacts. The grinding and pecking tool from Mali which was analysed confirms to a large degree the use-wear traits observed on similar American Indian, as well as on experimental cereal processing and re-sharpening tools. Yet, it also becomes clear that a much larger set of ethno-archaeological or experimental reference data is desirable, in order to refine the present results and to study the use-wear patterns on other types of rocks and artefacts.

Finally it would be important to look more closely at the social context in which these artefacts are used, considering the fact that in ethnographic contexts it is usually only women who use this type of tools. As most labour process regarding vegetal materials are traditionally related to women's work, the study of both tools and vegetal residues is one of the few ways to make these activities visible in the archaeological record. Moreover, many of these labour instruments are basic especially in agricultural societies, involving many hours of work. Apart from vegetable remains, residues can also form through the processing of ochre or other colourings, minerals, oils, etc. Macrolithic tools are essential for the reconstruction of these production processes and social life in general. Its systematic study would provide us with the possibility of analysing the forms and social organization of production, the productivity and amortization reached by the technical means of production, and the importance of different economic activities within the general production cycle of a society.

Acknowledgements

This work forms part of one of the research lines developed by the *Grup d'Arqueoecología Social Mediterrània*, supported by the C.I.R.I.T. of the *Generalitat de Catalunya* and the D.G.I.C.Y.T. of the *Ministerio de Educación y Ciencia*, Madrid. We wish to thank Alex Walker for his corrections of the English version.

Authors' addresses

Débora ZURRO
Becaria FI-DURSI (Generalitat de Catalunya)
Laboratori d'Arqueologia.Institució Milà i Fontanals – CSIC
Email: debora@bicat.csic.es

Roberto RISCH
Researcher of the *Ramón y Cajal* programme of the Spanish Ministery of Science and Technology
Dept. d'Antropologia Social i Prehistòria
Universitat Autònoma de Barcelona
Email: Robert.Risch@uab.es

Ignacio CLEMENTE CONTE
Laboratori d'Arqueologia.Institució Milà i Fontanals – CSIC
Email: ignacio@bicat.csic.es

Bibliography

ADAMS, J.L., 1988. Use-wear analyses on Manos and Hide-processing Stones. *Journal of Field Archaeology* 15: 307-315.

ADAMS, J.L., 1989. Methods for improving ground stone artifacts analysis: experiments in mano wear patterns. In: AMICK, D.S. & MAULDIN, R.P. (eds.), *Experiments in Lithic Technology*, B.A.R., Int.Ser., 528, Oxford: 259-281.

ADAMS, J.L., 1993. Mechanisms of wear of ground stone surfaces. *Pacific Coast Archaeological Society Journal* Quarterly 29(4): 60-73.

ADAMS, J.L., 1999. Refocusing the role of food-grinding tools as correlates for subsistence strategies in the U.S.Southwest. *American Antiquity* 64(3): 475-498.

ATCHINSON J. FULLAGAR R., 1998. Starch residues on pounding elements from Jinmium rock-shelter. In: FULLAGAR R. (ed.), *A closer look: recent Australian studies of stone tools*. Sydney University Archaeological Methods Series n. 6: 109-125.

BARTON H., TORRENCE R. & FULLAGAR R., 1998. Clues to stone tool function re-examined: comparing starch grain frequencies on used and unused obsidian artefacts. *Journal of Archaeological Science* 25: 1231-1238.

BEAUNE, S.A. de, 1989. Exemple ethnographique de l'usage plurifonctionel d'un galet de quartz. *Bulletin de la Société Préhistorique Française* 86,2: 61-65.

BÖHNER, U., 1997. Die Felssteingeräte der endneolithischen Siedlung von Dietfurt a.d. Altmühl, Lkr. Neumarkt i.d. Opf, Archäologie am Main-Donau Kanal, 10, Marie Leidorf, Espelkamp.

BROADBENT, N.D., 1979. *Coastal resources and settlement stability: a critical study of a Mesolithic Site Complex in Northern Sweden*. Uppsala University, Uppsala.

CASTRO, P., CHAPMAN, R., GILI, S., LULL, V., MICË, R., RIHUETE, C., RISCH, R. y SANAHUJA, M.E., 1999. *Proyecto Gatas 2. La dinámica arqueoecológica de la ocupación prehistórica.* Junta de Andalucía, Consejería de Cultura, Sevilla.

CLEMENTE CONTE, I., 1997. *Los instrumentos líticos de Túnel VII: una aproximación etnoarqueológica.* Treballs d'Etnoarqueologia 2, CSIC-UAB. Madrid.

CZAJA A.Th., 1978 Structure of starch grains and the classification of vascular plant families. *Taxon* 27(5/6), November 1978: 463-470.

ESAU K., 1978. *Anatomía vegetal.* 3ªed. Revisada. Ed. Omega, Barcelona.

GONZÁLEZ URQUIJO, J.E. & IBÁÑEZ ESTÉVEZ, J.J., 1994. *Metodología del análisis funcional de instrumentos tallados en sílex.* Cuadernos de Arqueología nº 14. Universidad de Deusto, Bilbao.

GRONENBORN, D., 1994. Ethnoarchäologische Untersuchungen zur rezenten Herstellung und Nutzung von Mahlsteinen in Nordost-Nigeria. *Experimentelle Archäologie Bilanz 1994*, Isensee, Oldenburg: 45-55.

HAYDEN, B., 1979. *Palaeolithic reflections: lithic technology and ethnographic excavations among Australian Aborigines.* Australian Institute of Aboriginal Studies, New Jersey.

HAYDEN, B. (ed.), 1987. *Lithic studies among the contemporary Highland Maya.* The University of Arizona Press, Tucson.

HORSFALL, G.A., 1987. Design Theory and Grinding Stones. In: B. HAYDEN (ed.), *Lithic studies among the contemporary Highland Maya*, University of Arizona Press, Arizona: 323-77.

KRAYBILL, N., 1977. Pre-agricultural tools for the preparation of foods in the Old World. In: I. REED (ed.), *Origins of agriculture*, Mouton, The Hague: 485-521.

LOY T., 1994. Methods in the analysis of starch residues on prehistoric stone tools. In: HATHER J.G., *Tropical archaeobotany: applications and new developments.* One World Archaeology n.12, Ed. Routledge. London: 86-114

PIPERNO D. RANERE A. HOLST I. HANSELL P., 2000. Starch grains reveal early root crop horticulture in the Panamanian tropical forest. *Nature* 407: 894-895.

RISCH, R., 1995. *Recursos naturales y sistemas de producción en el Sudeste de la Península Ibérica entre 3000 y 1000 ANE*, Tesis Doctoral de la Universidad Autónoma de Barcelona, Ed. Microfotográfica, Bellaterra.

RISCH, R., 2002. *Recursos naturales, medios de producción y explotación social. Un análisis económico de la industria lítica de Fuente Alamo (Almería), 2250-1400 ANE*, P. von Zabern, Mainz.

SEMENOV, S.A., 1981. *Tecnología prehistórica. Estudio de las herramientas y objetos antiguos a través de las huellas de uso*, Akal, Madrid.

SOBOLIK K.D. 1996. Lithic organic residue analysis: an example from the southwestern archaic. *Journal of Field Archaeology* 23: 461-469.

STARNINI, E. & VOYTEK, B., 1997. New lights on old stones: the ground stone assemblage from the Bernab_Brea excavation at Arene Candide. *Memorie dell'Istituto Italiano di Paleontologia Umana* V, pp. 427-511.

SUSSMAN, C., 1988. *A microscopic analysis of use-wear and polish formation on experimental quartz tools.* B.A.R., Int.Ser., 395, Oxford.

THERIN M., 1998. The movement of starch grains in sediments. In: FULLAGAR R. (edr.), *A closer look: recent Australian studies on stone tools.* Sydney University Archaeological Methods Series nº6: 61-72.

THERIN M., FULLAGAR R., TORRENCE R., 1999. Starch in sediments: a new approach to the study of subsistence and land use in New Guinea. In: GOSDEN CH. & HATHER J. (eds.), *The prehistory of food. Appetites for change.* One World Archaeology n.32, Ed. Routledge. London, pp. 438-462.

WRIGHT, K., 1992. A classification system for ground stone tools from the prehistoric Levant. *Paléorient* 18/2: 53-81.

ZIMMERMANN, A., 1988. Steine. In: BOELICKE, U. et al., *Der bandkeramische Siedlungsplatz Langweiler* 8, Gemeinde Aldenhoven, Kr. Düren, Rhein.Ausgrab. 28, Bonn.

www.ingramcontent.com/pod-product-compliance
Ingram Content Group UK Ltd.
Pitfield, Milton Keynes, MK11 3LW, UK
UKHW061213180426
11947UKWH00029B/2033